IMMORTALITY

THE INEVITABILITY OF ETERNAL LIFE

KABBALIST RAV BERG

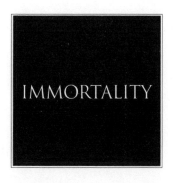

IMMORTALITY

KABBALIST RAV BERG

FOR MY WIFE

 AREN

IN THE VASTNESS OF TIME,
AND THE INFINITY OF SPACE,
IT IS MY GREAT BLISS AND
MY MOST TREASURED GIFT
TO SHARE A SOULMATE
WITH YOU.

For further information:

The Kabbalah Centre
Director Rav Berg

1-800-KABBALAH
www.kabbalah.com
14 Ben Ami St., Tel Aviv, Israel 63342
155 E. 48th, New York City, NY 10017
1062 S. Robertson Blvd., Los Angeles, CA 90035

Second Edition
August 2000
Printed in Canada

ISBN 1-57189-102-1

May the teachings of Kabbalah
lead us all into the new millennium,
bringing peace, love, health
and prosperity.

———•◆•———

I would like to dedicate Immortality to
my dear family and cherished friends.

———•◆•———

This book was dedicated
on the 24th of Cheshvan 5760
– death anniversary of
Rabbi Avraham Azulai

———•◆•———

Steven Mark Abrams

———•◆•———

Zevulun Ben Baruch

CONTENTS

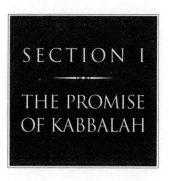

SECTION I

THE PROMISE
OF KABBALAH

"WHEN THE STUDENT
IS READY, THE TEACHER
SHALL APPEAR"

INTRODUCTION:
THE REALITY OF IMMORTALITY

The nagging notion that it's just too good to be true
is deeply ingrained in our consciousness.

Immortality has remained the coveted dream of mystics and explorers for millennia—among them, Ponce de Leon, the 16th century conqueror, who voyaged to many new worlds in quest of the Fountain of Youth. Though the fabled geyser eluded the Spanish explorer in his travels, Ponce de Leon did manage to discover Florida, which, ironically, now boasts miles of oceanfront motels teeming with senior citizens seeking to prolong their stay on this planet.

Then there was James Bedford, a 73-year-old psychologist from Glendale, California, who, in 1967, had his body frozen in a process known as cryogenics. This was an effort to keep his physical self intact until medical science discovers the magic elixir that will bring about the end of disease and the beginning of eternal life.

Nonetheless, if the average man or woman were offered the opportunity to live forever, they would very probably decline, frightened off by the prospect of deathlessness and all that it might entail: continuous financial turmoil, eternal marital strife, endless mortgage payments, and the perpetual pain of outliving loved ones. Why, they might ask, would anyone desire immortality and eternal life?

Sadly, many people view death as an escape from a cursed and chaos-stricken world that, all too often, feels more like a house of detention than a Garden of Eden. Some of us even believe that we are defined by our own mortality. The inevitability of death gives life meaning.

But the idea that "death is a natural part of living" is a trap. It stems partly from the notion that life is necessarily filled with turmoil, pain, and suffering, for that is all we really know. It's what we read about in newspapers; what we witness on television; what we experience in our day-to-day lives.

Chaos is so frequent and familiar that it feels like part of our family. If it's not a financial roller coaster, then it's a pill for our anxiety and depression. If it's not a rotten relationship torturing the soul, then it's a dreadful disease tormenting the body. Chaos has become an integral part of our existence. We've been conditioned to accept it. And we don't really want to say goodbye to it! We have a masochistic need to hold onto our problems—to cradle them in our arms, refusing to let them go. We have reached the point where peace of mind and tranquility are a shock to our system. Lasting fulfillment is unfamiliar territory, and fear of the unknown is our natural instinct.

We've been so battered and banged around by life

that we invariably look over our shoulder if things suddenly begin to work out for us. The nagging notion that it's just too good to be true is deeply ingrained in our consciousness. We've become complacent in our chaos, dispassionate about the prospect of positive change, and, worst of all, skeptical of solutions that might offer us a better way to live.

But life does not have to be like that. Life was never meant to be like that. And the concept of immortality, according to Kabbalah, is not defined solely as physical unending life. In truth, the quality of life is far more important than just the duration of it. Some people live and experience 70 years as though it were one long, routine day, while others live and experience one day as though it were 70 fulfilling years.

Though our first instinct may be to reject the following idea, make no mistake: Unending joy, everlasting tranquility, and eternal fulfillment are all part of the immortality concept. It's a package deal.

Immortality ultimately means the demise of the death force itself—the same death force that is responsible for the collapse of a good relationship, the death of a prosperous business, and the end of someone's happiness.

ANSWERS BEGIN WITH QUESTIONS

The visionaries who dared to contemplate and expound upon these intriguing but forbidden matters were known as Kabbalists.

In order to understand immortality, we must first begin questioning what life and death are all about. We must discern the meaning of our own existence. We must question all the pain and suffering that afflicts mankind and understand life's ultimate purpose.

Prior to my own introduction into the world of Kabbalah, I felt a deep yearning to explore these haunting and profound issues, but I was intensely frustrated at the lack of knowledge made available by organized religion. Compelling questions pertaining to immortality, life and death, pain and suffering, and the whereabouts of God when we need Him most, were not to be investigated by rabbinical authorities. In truth, my rabbinical contemporaries and I were just as much in the dark regarding the answers as the people to whom we were ministering.

As I would eventually find out, speculations of this nature were only to be found in an ancient body of knowledge that had remained tightly guarded and kept under wraps throughout human history— Kabbalah. The visionaries who dared to contemplate and expound upon these intriguing but forbidden matters were known as Kabbalists.

One of these eminent Kabbalists removed the blinders from my own eyes in an effort to awaken humanity from a 2000-year-old coma.

MY ENCOUNTERS WITH MY MASTERS

On a June day in 1962, I met my master, Rabbi Yehuda Brandwein. Who would have guessed that measured against all my triumphs and failures, this would prove to be the most important moment of my whole lifetime? How can we ever explain how one chance meeting with a person can leave such a signif-icant and lasting impression?

By the time I met him, my master had become famous by publishing the only translation and com-mentary on the "Tikune Zohar," out of an ancient, incomprehensible Aramaic into Hebrew. The Zohar contains the keys to Kabbalah, the mystical body of thought that connects the mysteries of this world with the mysteries of the divine. The Tikune Zohar is the section that contains all of the hidden laws of the universe that could not be revealed until our own day and age. The first work to contain these secrets was written some 4,000 years ago by the Biblical patriarch Avraham, but his work was too couched in difficult wording to be understood.

Some 2,000 years after Avraham, Rabbi Shimon bar Yochai, the grand master of Kabbalistic knowledge, created a more complete edition than that of his predecessor. Rabbi Shimon called the book, the Zohar, the Book of Splendor. This was a book of secrets concerning the very nature of reality—a guide to the "ascent of the soul." Although it was enlightening and informative, the Zohar was still limited because it was accessible to only a few people. The secrets of the universe hidden there were still waiting to be revealed, not just to Jews but to all of humanity, from the era that began in the final days of the 15th century, and continuing into our own time. These secrets are an enormous step forward in assisting us in ending the chaos that has ravaged humankind since time immemorial, and in finally achieving control over our existence here on earth.

The complete understanding of these secrets had to wait for the 20th century and my master, Rabbi Yehuda Brandwein, and his teacher, Rabbi Yehuda Ashlag. Kabbalah itself has been for too long a jealously guarded secret, locked up in an ancient vault. The time has finally come for it to reach out with its message of simplicity. In the final analysis, knowledge understood by the layperson is true knowledge. The science of Kabbalah answers many of the challenges posed by the enigmatic aspects of nature, and yet it remains simple. Kabbalists' vision of reality is based on an in-depth perception of the Bible's coded narration and tales. Kabbalah teachings provide the principles by which we can establish power and influence over our environment and by which we can understand the power that nature holds over us.

Since Adam and Eve, people have been helpless before this power; the reality that, sooner or later, what has come to be popularly known as Murphy's Law will take over. Murphy's Law states that if something can happen, it will. The careful orders we establish will disintegrate before the mounting pressures of our daily lives, and chaos will reign. Until now, no one could avoid chaos. If one was fortunate enough to escape the chaos of illness, then the chaos of financial ruin would set in, or the chaos of family crisis would take over. And of course, we cannot ignore the ultimate chaos, the final scenario: the mortality of the human body. Death.

KABBALAH BRIDGES THE GAP BETWEEN SCIENCE AND RELIGION

People of the modern world who had resigned themselves to existing in a spiritual vacuum now have an alternative.

My master, Rabbi Yehuda Brandwein and his teacher, Rabbi Yehuda Ashlag, allow us to now share this moment of witnessing and participating in a people's revolution of enlightenment. They are responsible for a dramatic shift in human consciousness. They received the divine instruction enabling them to show us how to change our attitudes. In doing so, they broke with a 4,000-year-old tradition of sealing the vital information of Kabbalah in an ancient, dusty vault. It is true that before them, other courageous Kabbalists, from the 16th century onward, crossed the borders of secrecy surrounding this life-enhancing compendium of knowledge. Perhaps the most famous was Rabbi Moses Luzatto. For daring to confront tradition, these people faced daily harassment. They were ostracized, mentally abused, and beaten by the keepers of the faith. They were made outcasts. They were forced to leave Jerusalem. So it is not surprising that my master and his teacher were also cast out for breaking with tradition, for daring to make Kabbalah accessible to the layperson. The conventional, organized system within Judaism reacted to them with abuse, intolerance, and sometimes violence.

I was groomed, from early childhood, to be a conventional rabbi. This was the tradition, and I grew up within the framework of this time-honored, sometimes antiquated, tradition that had not met the new challenges of a rapidly changing civilization. Particularly, advances in science—from relativity and space travel, to breakthroughs in medicine such as genetic engineering, to the computer revolution of our information age—have exaggerated the chasm between formal religion and people who refuse to deny the reality of the modern world.

In the past, when science was on a collision course with religious doctrine, scientists such as Galileo and Copernicus were sometimes coerced into disavowing their new discoveries. But our present time is different. The gap between science and religion has grown so deep and wide that people have had to choose between being in one world or the other. Now along come my master and his teacher, whose teachings bridge this gap by actually promoting the principles of Newtonian and quantum physics that the scientific establishment embraces. The divine sources—the ancient Kabbalists—understood these same principles long before either religious or scientific traditions became systems. Kabbalah anticipated science, and science is only now catching up with Kabbalah. People of the modern world who had resigned themselves to existing in a spiritual vacuum now have an alternative.

Because I have been given to understand all this, it is not surprising that I, too, have been attacked for breaking with tradition. Yet I recall a story of my master and his teacher. When Rabbi Yehuda Brandwein was still a young man, he lived far from his master,

Rabbi Yehuda Ashlag. Each day Rabbi Brandwein took an hour-long bus ride to study with his teacher, but when zealots found out about his studies, they arranged for Brandwein to be refused entrance to the bus. Did this deter my master in his mission of learning how, at last, to bring Kabbalah to the people, how finally to bring peace to the wars between science and religion? On the contrary, Rabbi Yehuda Brandwein could be seen walking for two or three hours each day to be with his master.

And so I, too, cannot be deterred. I cannot deny the significance of my chance meeting with my master in 1962. I have before me the example of brave Kabbalists who risked their lives to reveal the hidden secrets of Kabbalah. I have by chance arrived at the very moment those secrets were destined to be revealed. My mission is to bring to you at last the actualization of what before was only potential. My mission is to realize the promise of Kabbalah. I have been privileged to arrive at a radically new vantage point whose coordinates were prepared by many before me. This book shares the way many familiar things look from this new vantage point, and they look very different. The stories of Adam and Eve, of Moses and the Golden Calf, of the Diaspora and the Holocaust, all of these events appear very different when looked upon with a new understanding.

THE "WHY" OF THINGS

*The most significant change of modern times
is this revolution of the mind.*

Kabbalah goes beyond bridging the chasm between science and religion. It acknowledges something that science and religion have failed to address— namely, the "why" of things. In the Zohar, Rabbi Shimon bar Yochai specifically states that the information offered in his work was never to be accepted simply because he was the author. The "why" of everything must be stated and the answers to every "why" must be forthcoming before the teachings can be embraced.

Kabbalah does not merely seek to understand the mechanics of how things function; it provides insights into why things are as they are. Rather than accepting the conclusions of science as fact, Kabbalah insists that a thinking person ask why a particular condition exists in the first place. Tradition—adherence to practices and methods merely because they have always been followed—has given way to the scrutiny of the individual. More people are concerned now with the "why" of things than with the "how."

In the 21st century, people are beginning to question everything as never before. Indeed, the most significant change of modern times is this revolution of the mind. Perhaps this is due to advances in science. With the development of modern physics and quantum mechanics, visual reality has become suspect. Things are no longer what they seem to be. When we look at the stars in the sky, we now know that we are seeing some distant stars not as they are now, but as they were when their light first began to travel toward us. When we look at a table that appears to be solid, we know that if we could see the table with sufficient magnification, we would discover that on an atomic level, it is not solid at all. And when we see a photograph, we are uncertain if the image represents the real face of a person or if it is a face "corrected" by digital techniques so that it bears no imperfections.

When we begin to question, we have begun to transform our nature. For millennia, people have been stuck in a reactive mode, emotionally, mentally, and physically, when it concerned the chaos and turmoil of existence. But now people are becoming proactive. Instead of behaving like sitting ducks, without anyone to shoot back at, we are learning to put what appears to be a chaotic event into proper perspective.

Consider the words of physicist Sir James Jeans, a Nobel laureate who stated that physical reality as we know it is but an interference pattern. Once this idea has been accepted, our search for the truth becomes paramount. We leave fear behind, for things are in fact different than how they initially appeared. We begin to realize that often the invisible things are the most enduring and important. Although much emphasis has been placed on the physical realm, science has drawn new attention to the unseen plane that we normally do not observe in our day-to-day life, but where all things start. This is the plane of Kabbalah.

Let us take something as simple as moving our fingers. Do these physical parts of the body decide to move by themselves, or is there a hidden consciousness that directs them? For that matter, is there any daily reality that has not originated as thought? Over the centuries, humanity and science became so involved in the physical, material realm that the cause and essential design of consciousness took a back seat. But now physics has changed all that.

THE LIGHT OF THE CREATOR

All religions have their Kabbalists.

Why did science have to wait until the 20th century to penetrate the secrets of the universe? The answer is simple: Rabbi Ashlag lived in the 20th century. His efforts were necessary to unveil the subconscious realm of the universe by revealing the concealed wisdom of Kabbalah, and thus, turning on the Light, the Light of Kabbalah. The veils, limitations, and illusions of the conscious mind then began to disappear. The Light began to take its rightful place in our universe. This prompted the remarkable and wondrous theories, discoveries, and new technological achievements with which we have been blessed. The limitations of the physical world—time, space, and motion—are falling away.

How could something so immense be so simple? If we think of electric light, we can understand the sudden transformation. A mere flip of the light switch transforms a dark room, whether it be a tiny closet or an immense auditorium. This act of turning on the Light, so central in Kabbalah, is recognized in all spiritual teachings. All religions have their Kabbalists.

Humanity has been pondering the Zohar for millennia, trying to unravel its secrets, to demystify its codes. But there has been little or no success. In the 20th century, Rabbi Ashlag removed the cloak and unveiled the mysteries. And when the Light goes on, previously unrealized and unseen discoveries are noticed. They were there all the time—we just could not see them.

This comparison between the immense power of the Zohar's illumination and an ordinary light switch was made to me by my master. He explained that when the power of Kabbalah is unleashed into the cosmos, things that we did not know existed suddenly appear before our eyes. We do not trip over the furniture in a darkened room once the light goes on. So, too, as we stumble through life's journey, falling, becoming bedridden, not knowing what to do, we can find a simple solution to our problems. We can just turn on the light, and the interference of this physical realm disappears.

BRINGING THE LIGHT TO ALL PEOPLE

"Rabbi Brandwein has become the perfect human being, in all his dignity, existing beyond social status or religion."
—*Secretary General of the Histadrut*

After Rabbi Ashlag created his path-breaking translation of a major section of the Zohar, he went on to write a 16-volume textbook. For the first time, a layperson could systematically explore this previously hermetic discipline. This was a great step forward in bringing the Light out of the locked vault. Some attacked this daring move. Still, Rabbi Ashlag and Rabbi Brandwein did not yet go against all the rules. They still maintained the traditional restrictions regarding who could receive this newly designed education in Kabbalah. Only men over the age of 40 were permitted to attend classes. Furthermore, they had to have already advanced through a Talmudic education. They had to be observant Orthodox Jews. In addition, their knowledge of Jewish law was tested with extreme scrutiny to determine whether they were fully knowledgeable in every facet of Judaic laws and customs.

Another requirement was the students' "certainty of heart." Only those who experienced a longing that could be filled solely with the teachings of Kabbalah were welcome. The students were also required to remain apart from people who were atheists or irreligious, so as to not be polluted. Even as I write this, there are still many sects within Judaism that maintain these traditional prohibitions against mingling with strangers.

In the face of this closed attitude, Rabbi Brandwein was to take yet another step in opening the hearts and minds of the people to the Light of Kabbalah. He breached the sacrosanct restrictions regarding students and practitioners of Kabbalah when he formally accepted a position as Chief Rabbi of the one million strong labor organization in Israel known as the "Histadrut." The Histadrut annual dinner and dance took place on the holiest of holy days, Yom Kippur, a day revered by most Jews, religious and non-religious.

Rabbi Brandwein was thus serving as the religious leader of an organization that broke the rules in an extreme way. Such a provocative action on the part of Rabbi Brandwein created an uproar in all traditional circles, whether Orthodox, Conservative, or Reform. Here was a rabbi garbed in traditional clothing, certainly not from the circle of nonbelievers, amid an atheistic Israeli organization. Even more alarming was the fact that he was a Kabbalist, required to maintain the highest degree of purity and withdraw from any suspect contacts with the outside world. I remember well the fears of his wife: her children might never marry, since no traditional family would dream of having their children enter into marriage with the children of such a heretical rabbi!

The true significance of my master's acceptance of this position with the Histadrut was not yet clear to me. He was in fact establishing the groundwork for what was to be a complete and definitive break with Kabbalistic tradition. His teacher, Rabbi Ashlag, had been destined to open the sealed vaults and make the teachings of Kabbalah accessible to the masses. Rabbi Brandwein would in turn become the first Kabbalist to actually go out among the people. At Histadrut conferences he shared the principles of Kabbalah without benefit of lectures. Sometimes it is most effective to go in through the back door!

The appearance of Rabbi Brandwein dispelled the notion that he was anything but Orthodox. How in the world could the people of this organization feel comfortable in his presence? Yet what I witnessed was nothing short of a miracle. I saw heretics and anti-religionists actually embracing my master with a love I had never seen before. Somehow, here was tolerance and sensitivity between very different people. Although at the time I was mystified by such harmony, the profound lessons I learned from these encounters remain with me to this day.

Once, when my master was scheduled to meet with the secretary-general of the Histadrut, I asked to be taken along. I was yearning to find out why such a group would have chosen him. There were certainly other candidates who appeared to more appropriately fulfill the group's objectives, rabbis who represented a much more liberal approach to Jewish religious law.

As it turned out, the leader of the Histadrut had origins in a long line of the ultra-religious right; yet he was now so alienated from his background that he despised the very existence of religion. When I asked him my simple question, I received a simple, shocking answer.

He stated matter-of-factly that Rabbi Brandwein was not a rabbi at all. No, Rabbi Brandwein was a Kabbalist. This was the very first time I had heard anyone make such a distinction. I could not yet understand it and asked him for an explanation.

Again his response startled me. "Why can't you understand what I am trying to say? It is so simple. Rabbi Brandwein has become the perfect human being, in all his dignity, existing beyond social status or religion. Jew or non-Jew, sick or poor, a person of high position or lowly status—to Rabbi Brandwein these distinctions mean nothing. For him we are all human beings, and our souls are part of the Creator. He holds the value of loving his neighbor as high and unconditionally as he holds the actual observance of his religion."

Such an experience is unforgettable. I gradually began to understand why the workers in the Histadrut responded so warmly to my master. They felt, in a direct and undeniable way, the clear and compassionate Light within him. I remembered my own sensation at that first chance meeting with my master. My own background had not been in Kabbalah, and it had dictated that I keep a good distance from such mystical subjects. Yet when I met my master, the sensation can only be described as a kind of physical melting away. This is the power of Kabbalah. I could actually feel my soul being touched by my master, as if his warm, wonderful hands were comforting me.

After witnessing my teacher among the Histadrut,

my work and personal life henceforth had a new master—the uncompromising principle of unconditional love, sensitivity, and tolerance for everything God has brought into existence, be it flower or weed, human being, or ant.

SCIENCE ADVANCES BUT THE SATAN RULES

My intention is to bring about an awareness that chaos of whatever kind is the work of the Satan.

"Why are we here?" is a question that has haunted the minds of human beings since the dawn of human consciousness. Kabbalah tells us that before the origins of the physical world, the infinite energy and Light of the Creator filled eternity. The essence of this energy was boundless beneficence, fulfillment, and sharing. To manifest sharing, the Light created an infinite Vessel, which includes all the souls of humankind, to receive that which the Creator imparted. In the process, the Vessel inherited traits of the Creator and therefore felt unfulfilled at receiving so much without being able to be the cause. So we, the Vessel, came here to earn the fulfillment through the action of choosing Light over Darkness. To aid us, the Light created the angel, The Satan, to test us and give us free will. Just as the domain of Light exists, so also there exists the domain of darkness. This domain has been recognized from time immemorial. Its emperor has been given the name of "the Satan" by people of religion, and people of science have called him "entropy" or "Murphy," the master of Murphy's Law. By any name, the Satan unleashes evil and chaos into the universe, and the last thing that this emperor of the dark world wants is to have his dark kingdom disappear when the Light goes on. Throughout the history of humankind, the Satan has been threatened by the Light whenever it has penetrated into his dark domain.

He has known for a long time that with the spread of Kabbalah, the world and its people would be enlightened. And so, when Rabbi Ashlag and Rabbi Brandwein acted as jump-starters for the Light to go on throughout the universe, it rubbed the Satan the wrong way. He fought back, unleashing a barrage of unreasonable, illogical energies into the cosmos to be picked up and channeled by evil people of all sorts.

This is how the cosmic struggle between good and evil has found its way into our familiar world of existence. The battle lines are drawn. Against the Satan's final play for empirical power, Kabbalists Rabbi Ashlag and Rabbi Brandwein had fired the first salvo. They understood that the information of Kabbalah must be within the grasp of the laypeople, for without popular participation, the Satan would still remain supreme, as he has throughout history.

But this action provoked the Satan to seek out more evil people to carry out his dark mission of chaos. He knew he could keep the world's population in check through evil dictators and even presidents, who throughout the millennia have left human rubble in the landscapes of history. It has been easy for him to spread chaos: nationalism alone has been sufficient to deny almost any country lasting peace and contentment.

And of course, for good measure, the Satan has thrown in disease, plagues, floods, and earthquakes. With all this chaos and distraction, no one would know he was the real culprit behind all of our problems. For what would the faithful do? They would see all this chaos as part of God's plan. But why should virtuous people be subject to the actions of the wicked? The faithful reply, "God, in His mysterious ways, knows what He is doing. Who are we to question God?"

THE SATAN IN GOD'S CLOTHING

If I believed the chaos and disasters we are seeing today were the work of God, I would agree. But why would a kind, compassionate God have an evil thought-consciousness, let alone punish the innocent and then permit the criminal to go free? He does not, and those who think He does are dressing the Satan in

God's clothing. And of course, he is happy to be silent about the disguise.

What about the nonbelievers, those who either reject the notion of an Almighty or simply pay no attention to a God? Well, the Satan has devised his cloak of protection for these people as well, by fooling the whole world with two words: lucky and unlucky. When people get cancer, we say they are unlucky. Those who remain healthy are the lucky. When a 10-year-old dies, we say that he has suffered a lack of luck. When a 110-year-old dies, we say that she has been blessed with an abundance of luck. Whatever happens, the Satan fools us, for the one thing he fears most is the possibility of the Light removing the glory of his dark kingdom, the ultimate sign of his power and dominion—decay and death. The idea of immortality makes the Satan shudder.

My intention is to bring about an awareness that chaos—of whatever kind—is the work of the Satan. If we find peaceful solutions, he is out of the business of creating chaos and making it manifest. Throughout history, including the time of the Exodus with Moses, the Satan has deployed his bag of tricks—tricks that have worked for him around the clock, throughout the year, since the beginning. He has securely locked the idea of mortality into the consciousness of the people. Since Adam and Eve, we have thought of mortality as a permanent fixture, an inevitable part of life on Earth. And so, until the 21st century, the Satan has been complacent.

THE PEOPLE'S REVOLUTION OF ENLIGHTENMENT

We have just entered a new millennium, when good things are supposed to happen. It is true that we witnessed extraordinary changes during the 20th century. We have accepted technological advances never dreamed of only a century ago. The telephone has removed the barrier of physical distance. Inventions—from washing machines to automobiles to computers—have provided humankind with more leisure time. The tourist-leisure industry flourishes as it has at no other time in history. Why, then, is so little change noticeable in our daily living experiences?

Despite advanced medical research, diseases and viruses that were once believed to be extinct are returning in increasingly stubborn strains. During the past century, medical research has taken credit for the sharp decline in infectious diseases such as cholera, polio, and tuberculosis. But after believing that most of these diseases had almost ceased to exist, today we find that they are on the upswing.

Thomas McKlown, a leading specialist in the field

of public health and social medicine, has provided sufficient proof that the striking decline in mortality has not been the result of medical intervention alone. There have been other contributing factors, including improvements in hygiene, sanitation, and nutrition. McKlown's study showed that major infectious diseases had all peaked and begun to decline long before medical researchers had developed effective combatant medications and immunization techniques.

It appears that medical intervention alone cannot bring about significant changes in basic disease patterns. Thus, while there has been progress in unraveling biological factors involved in specific diseases, and in developing technologies that will affect them, identifying and labeling the disease is not necessarily equivalent to progress in health care. Of course, there has been remarkable progress in dealing with acute infection, premature births, procedures relating to organ transplants and open-heart surgery, and emergency medical practices of all kinds. But these spectacular medical advances do not tell us why the conditions necessitating them arose in the first place, or what measures might have prevented them from occurring. This book is not intended as a criticism of medical practices or personnel, but I do wish to show that conventional medicine fails to address health concerns at their core.

When I asked my master to what we can attribute the sudden rise in the life expectancy of humankind, I was taken aback by his curt response: "It is related to the influence of the time in which we live."

THE NEW MILLENNIUM

Only through the teachings and knowledge of the Zohar can humankind ever hope to eliminate chaos and mortality from the physical realm.

The emperor of evil had paid no attention when a certain young, unassuming rabbi provided laypeople with the text of Kabbalah in a version that, finally, could be understood. However, when Rabbi Brandwein brought Kabbalah to the people, he truly ended the Satan's complacency. The Satan had known of and been pleased with all the restrictions placed on exactly who could study Kabbalah. He never before had to fear he might lose his job, but now all that was about to change.

This change is the appearance of the new millennium. As a new era dawns, it transforms our vision of the past. Some of the most terrible things that have happened in the last 500 years are beginning to be seen in retrospect as the shudderings and shakings of a great transformation. This is the change ushered in by our own time, the age of the people's enlightenment. Now the Light of Kabbalah escapes from the dusty vault and illumines the world. Many wise men of the past had seen it coming. I am not the first to recognize that Kabbalah must be a popular movement in order to bring about the necessary change. From the year 1540, the year of Rabbi Isaac Luria's induction into the world of Kabbalah, and onwards, there was a strong recommendation that everyone—man, woman, and child—turn to the study of Kabbalah. Only through the teachings and knowledge of the Zohar could humankind ever hope to achieve the elimination of chaos and mortality from the physical realm. In 1614, in his treatise The Light of the Sun, Rabbi Avraham Azulai declared that all people, young and old, should study Kabbalah.

Yet until now, the time and environment were not ripe, nor was the cosmos opened sufficiently for Kabbalistic revelation. I see it as having begun to open in 1490, when the Jews of Spain were suddenly forced into exile. This was a very significant date. Things seemed to be stable around the globe. There seemed to be no need to prepare for the attack that the Satan would suddenly unleash, chaos such as had been known only some 1,500 years before, when the Temple was destroyed. At that time, whole nations of people were displaced, as would be the case in 1490, and again in 1940.

When the upheaval and displacement of people

took place in 1490, the people began to question their control over the environment and their own lives. If there is one desire all people share, it is to have a settled life. The thought of exile created great anxiety. The consciousness of humanity was forced to break out of its slumbering, state of illusionary security. We were allowed to see our existence as it really was: chaotic and headed toward death.

When we are settled, we can still latch onto our little world and find some solace there—the sense that we are still essentially in control. When we are forced to leave the country against our will, however, any semblance of mastery over our destiny is destroyed.

Yet paradoxically, it is only when we lose control that we are forced to recognize the superior position of our opponent the Satan. That recognition is the key to achieving victory over him. The Spanish Inquisition made us aware of our true position in relation to the Satan. The day that Kabbalah knowledge and consciousness would become widespread was stirring and demanding freedom, but the people were not fully ready. Only further chaos and a complete loss of identity would entirely forge the crucible for a real transformation. Those Jews for whom displacement was more cruel than death would opt for a complete obliteration of their identity by connecting to Christianity. Yet whether by displacement or conversion, a realization of not being in control was essentially achieved. The opportunity to arrive at a hopeless and helpless state of existence was provided by the entrance of the age of exploration, when boundaries would be shaken and new worlds would be both found and destroyed.

The Spaniards proceeded on a rampage of world dominion, seeking to extend their reign throughout the world. They invaded North America, where they successfully brought on the chaos they never knew was their destiny. The Satan was at the height of his glory. Little did he realize that the chaos he so gleefully stood by and watched was a double-edged sword. Assuredly, the Jews in Spain, as well as the entire native populations of Mexico, South America, and later the Pacific, were undergoing pain and suffering. However, at the same time, the smug, self-contained state of consciousness that the Satan had built up over the past 1,500 years was beginning to show signs of cracking. The persecutions endured by the people were taking their toll. Anguish and helplessness had left their mark on the earth's inhabitants, and changes were now eagerly being sought. The door had been opened. For the first time, people were prepared to accept a dramatic shift in their way of thinking.

THE THINGS THAT LAST

There is an essence of which humankind has long been unaware.

The final tally is not yet in. For now, in the 21st century, we can appreciate that changes in the invisible world are gradual. They do not take place overnight, as I have painfully learned. It is the Kabbalist who studies how the entire universe—physical and metaphysical, celestial and terrestrial—has been, is, and will be influenced and determined by the consciousness and activity of humankind. The way of Kabbalah may evolve in a gradual process over millennia. We are speaking of the things that last, not of things that are here today and gone tomorrow. There is an essence of which humankind has long been unaware. Humankind has been blind to its presence. This essence is the Light force of God.

ADAM AND EVE: A NEW PERSPECTIVE

Remain connected with the Tree of Life reality and be sure of immortality.

So much has to do with our choice of the kind of reality with which we want to connect. Everyone recalls the Bible stories about Adam and Eve in the Garden, together with the nemesis of the universe— the snake, also known as the Satan. God had instruct- ed Adam and Eve not to eat from the Tree of the

Knowledge of Good and Evil, for they would surely die. They were, however, permitted to eat from the Tree of Life. When the snake approached Adam and Eve and asked them why they did not eat from the Tree of Knowledge, they responded that the Lord forbade them to eat from this tree, for they would surely die. The snake responded, "Don't be silly. Eat from it and you shall see that you will not die."

And lo and behold, when they did eat from the Tree of Knowledge, they did not die. Adam lived to the age of 930 years. What the Satan did not reveal to them was that once they ate from the Tree of Knowledge, they fell under his dominion and were subject to the satanic law of mortality. This was the warning of the Lord: "Connect to the Tree of Knowledge and you shall ultimately die—although not necessarily now. Remain connected with the Tree of Life reality and be sure of immortality."

THE THIRD TIME IS THE CHARM: ADAM AND EVE, THE GOLDEN CALF, AND NOW

Humankind must recognize a force in the universe that supersedes and reigns over the material world.

There have only been two "moments" when human beings were connected to the Tree of Life reality. The first occurred in the Garden of Eden, before

Adam fell from grace. After this fall, immortality ceased to be a viable force in the universe. People's programming changed and they lost consciousness of the supreme value of the spirit. They considered the material world to be the important arena of action, the place where people achieve their goals.

Then along came Moses, and the second "moment" came along with him. Moses, the Superman of his generation—the one who could accomplish anything and everything and have dominion over the material world—restored to the people the consciousness of humankind's dominion over the material world. But this "moment" lasted for only 40 days, while Moses was on Mount Sinai.

The idea that Moses shared with the Israelites at the time of the Exodus was the following: Human beings must recognize a force in the universe that supersedes and reigns over the material world. The Light of the Creator must be properly and harmoniously applied to the material world of our daily existence. Then people become the equivalent of God and, consequently, can assume the consciousness that has dominion over every aspect of the physical realm.

While people think that the material, physical world rules them, there can be no hope of their achieving an elevated state of consciousness over the visual, material world. People must realize that they are indeed capable of controlling the physical environment and all it contains. If this realization comes about, the application of the Light force with the secret codes of Kabbalah achieves for the practitioner nothing short of miracles and dominion over chaos.

This power, Moses demonstrated to the people on several memorable occasions. These were the marvels of his time, when he turned all the waters of Egypt— "its rivers, its canals, its ponds, all its bodies of water"—into blood, within sight of Pharaoh and his court. This power was demonstrated again in all the plagues that the Light force, through the blazing circuit of Moses, brought down upon Egypt. But Pharaoh was thinking only short-term. He looked only at the visual evidence of his eyes, and wanted only to have each plague removed. He thought it was all a matter of spells and hocus-pocus, and did not realize that the point was not whether frogs were in his bed or insects in his field or cattle dying in his pastures, but the long-term point was the power of the Light force. Finally, Pharaoh, who was no match for the power of the Light force, relented and the people were brought out to the land of milk and honey.

On the way, however, when they were in the desert, Moses needed to receive the Light of immortality. And while he was gone, the people became impatient. They began to lose their faith when they saw that Moses took so long to come back from Mount Sinai. You know the story—Moses' brother, Aaron, made them a Golden Calf out of all their worldly wealth, their gold earrings and rings. They reverted to the former prevailing consciousness that the material, physical world—the Golden Calf—is the main power that reigns over the human consciousness.

That's when the tablets of Light force energy shattered and when mortality again returned, its second chance spent. The Satan won out again, and he's still winning.

And so now, when we begin to sense that there must be more to life than material things, it's still difficult to consider replacing the material powers with such a metaphysical, supernatural, immaterial entity as the Light force. However, we now have a third chance, and the third time's the charm.

THE GOLDEN OPPORTUNITY OF DIASPORA AND THE LIGHT OF RABBI ISAAC LURIA

The dominion of the physical, material world is a very tough reign to break. In fact, nothing short of wholesale displacement is enough to shock people out of their forgetfulness of the memory of immortality.

Paradoxically, it is as if they must relive the trauma of Adam's removal from the Garden of Eden in order to re-enter that Garden.

While the mass displacements of populations that began in the late 15th century continued into the modern day, the revealing of the secrets of Kabbalah kept pace. In 1528, a child was born who was destined to shed light on the mysteries of the Light force and bring about the first comprehensive understanding of Kabbalah. His name was Isaac Luria. In 1540, as a recluse on the river Nile, he was already investigating the secrets of the universe. There is no doubt among Kabbalists that the Ari—the Lion, as he was called, was brought into this world to balance the torment that was being unleashed on earth.

The hundreds of students who gathered around the Ari became knowledgeable in the secrets. The knowledge and the practice encouraged the entrance of the Light force into the universe. However, the teachings were extremely difficult to understand and, as a result, the people were excluded from beneficial powers. Select individuals in each generation up until the 20th century, however, would maintain some balance and harmony in the world. It was the same world that was driven by humankind's intolerance and cruelty, and without these enlightened individuals, the world might have ended in complete destruction.

At the time Rabbi Ashlag appeared upon the scene, the battle lines favored the Satan. Still smacking his lips from the human carnage of a senseless World War I, which he had brought about through the assassination of one person, the Satan simply could not believe how gullible and asleep the consciousness of humankind had become. The world had been drawn into a chaotic war that had maimed and killed millions of innocent people. They were now being taught the work of the Satan: to destroy human life and property.

THE SATAN AND THE MODERN AGE

The Satan was reaping the rewards of millennia of hard work. He no longer had to employ his usual efforts or command the enormous resources of his army of evil entities. As he entered into the modern age, people did still suffer the usual forms of chaos that were his specialty—earthquakes, plagues, landslides, volcanic eruptions, drought, and so forth. But as the weapons of destruction became more and more powerful, his load lessened. As the nuclear era dawned, he realized that with a single stroke, he could bring about devastation that would not only involve the entire world, but would in turn create economic hardship that would be grounds for more wars that would feed upon themselves like malignant cancer cells. There was little doubt that the Satan's ultimate dream—the death of all humanity—would become a reality sooner than he had expected. More importantly, the consciousness of humanity had now approached a level where such annihilation seemed merited.

THE SATAN WEAVES SCIENTIFIC ADVANCEMENT INTO THE FABRIC OF UNCERTAINTY

Cloning was the crowning glory of the superhuman mind of man.

While all this destruction was coming about, humankind was making remarkable scientific progress that appeared to promise complete command over the material world. The limitations of time, space, and motion no longer held. People could fly in the skies and walk in space. The boundaries of communication came down. The medical establishment was making extraordinary breakthroughs and reaping equally large rewards. And finally, a feat with the most explosive and far-reaching implications was achieved—the cloning of another living entity, a sheep. Never since the birth of Adam had such an event occurred. This achievement was the crowning glory of the superhuman mind of man.

Yet the Satan hardly took this evidence of humanity's command over the universe as a sign to retreat to his war room and think he was back to square one. No, he was confident that he had his finger on the universal pulse. Gazing into his crystal ball, he could see into the future. What he observed was very gratifying to him. Humans, with all of their technological advancements, still had not learned how to live harmoniously with their neighbors. The Satan knew that this was the hidden secret, the key for unlocking the mysteries of immortality. He was reassured by the knowledge of the ultimate weapons in his arsenal for world domination—nuclear warheads and germ warfare—which promised to complete his triumph over physical existence, and demonstrate, once and for all, the magnitude of his power of death-consciousness.

Why would the Satan worry? He was able to keep playing his tricks, even in the face of two potentially threatening developments: 1) the efforts of my teacher and his teacher before him, and 2) the simultaneous unprecedented development of human technology, which promised to reshape the very nature of the material world. In regard to the former, Rabbi Ashlag had written a 16-volume textbook elucidating the study of Kabbalah. In 1922, he had also founded the Kabbalah Centre in Jerusalem, then known as the Yeshiva Bit Upland Le-Rabbanim, with the blessing of

Israel's first Chief Rabbi, Avraham Kook.

Regarding the second development, the information age of computers and the Internet brought the entire world as near as a local phone call. The Satan knew, however, that the cocoon environment of video games and e-mail was contrary to the sense of human community and mutuality that is necessary for his defeat.

Furthermore, the trump card the Satan produced and played in the game of science shows how clever an opponent he is: He introduced the so-called uncertainty principle into the heart of the scientific establishment. It was a masterpiece, a true work of art. The Satan wove scientific advancement into the fabric of uncertainty.

Yes, the Satan thought he did not need to be concerned. For despite technological advances and the appearance of Rabbi Ashlag, all around him he saw the continuation of his triumphs. He saw a human holocaust, with millions of people suffering poverty, starvation, disease, and the outright slaughter of war. For when it comes to the bottom line, has the quality of our lives really improved? Are financial institutions not rife with the traumas of restructuring, bankruptcy, and new levels of risk for financial disaster? Have we cured the torments of the homeless, the abused, the mentally ill, the drug addicted? Have we eased pain and chaos or defeated death? Have we conquered the Satan's forces and removed the final nemesis of mortality?

As if all this weren't enough to make the Satan lick his chops, the trick he has been using for millennia has still been working for him. His ingenious art of allowing humankind the illusion of control over chaos is as magical as ever.

WORLD POLITICS: MORE TRICKS OF THE SATAN

We generally disregard the fact that we are here in this universe for a limited time only.

This is the game the Satan plays with us all the time. He'll toss some small dose of chaos at us and then permit us to remove the chaos, and thus lead our consciousness into believing we are in control of physical reality. Near-death experiences are the Satan's most delightful ruse. An illusionary confidence overcomes us and we become oblivious to the reality of death.

Our behavior toward our fellow humans shows his hand. We generally disregard the fact that we are here in this universe for a limited time only. Were we to consider the fact of mortality, our attitudes would assume another character. We would behave differently in disagreements and arguments. We would forsake hatred and intolerance. If humankind realized that the chaos of mortality was a demonstration of the Satan's will, then, I believe, we would no longer be so concerned about what is wrong with others and would pay more attention to what might be wrong with ourselves.

Following World War I, the Satan was behind humankind's failure to worry that chaos might strike again. No one took notice of the dangerous bickering among nations following the victory over aggressors. The "common enemy"—an old trick of the Satan's!—had allowed humankind to forget that innocent people always bear the brunt of war, and after the war, the common cause disappears as if it had never existed. The Satan is back at work again, intensifying the differences between people and their intolerance of those differences. The Satan can manipulate leaders of nations without their even knowing who is behind their sudden about-face with former allies. The Satan provides the appropriate reasoning so that we never achieve the definitive victory over him—unity and tolerance between people.

Even the Holocaust of World War II did not allow us to see through the Satan's game. His strategy is always the same: 1) Shower the entire world with as much chaos as possible without letting on that he is behind it all, 2) present the chaotic package in such a way that humankind will not attribute the chaos to its rightful owner, 3) after the war, continue working in the form of isolationism and financial catastrophe, and 4) cause us to attribute the problems to others and not ourselves. The moment we realize that we are responsible for colluding in the chaos around us, then we have stepped onto the bridge to immortality.

THE QUARRELS OF KABBALISTS

Anyone reading and studying the content of the Zohar would assuredly go crazy and wind up in a mental institution.

The fact that former allies were already at each other's throats at the end of World War II was gratifying to the Satan. He also noted, with some discomfort, the developments among Kabbalists. He became aware that certain individuals were gathering intelligence on how to beat him at his own game.

Now he shifted into high gear. He employed the same strategy that had worked for him in the 18th century against the famous Kabbalist Rabbi Moses Luzatto. He enrolled scholars of the Bible and the Talmud to ban any Kabbalistic texts so they would not fall into the hands of learned laypeople. The word spread quickly. To strengthen their positions, the Satan impregnated the minds of these so-called authorities with scare tactics. Anyone reading and studying the content of the Zohar would assuredly go crazy and wind up in a mental institution, they said. The books were too holy for the average person to even touch. There were already other (non-Kabbalistic) books that were far simpler and could better benefit the reader. Because these so-called scholars spoke with authority, the entire world listened intently and with sub-servience. The Satan was very effective once again. The criticism of these authorities was so outlandish that one wonders when in the history of scholarship the opposition had been so intense and the facts so incorrect.

I INHERIT THE LEARNING CENTRE; KAREN OPENS IT TO ALL

My mission is to spread and disseminate this knowledge to every human being, in whatever language, in whatever country.

I recall the day that my master passed from the realm of the living in the year 1969. He was as cheer-ful as always, without as much as a hint that he would be leaving this familiar existence. We chatted all that day about the future of the Centre. All that he could tell me was, "I'm going to need tremendous support for whatever undertaking we embark upon." At that time, I was sure that my master was referring to moral and financial support from the community at large. He assured me that this would be forthcoming in ways unimaginable. Little did I realize that what my master was alluding to was his own death that would open the door to a previously unbelievable, impossible, and yet wonderful, reality of existence.

When my master passed on, I felt as if the rug had been pulled out from under me. In 1967, he had designated me as his successor, but I had hardly considered the enormity of what it would mean to be at the helm of the Kabbalah Learning Centre. In 1965, we had moved out of the small location in Israel and established the first branch of the Centre in New York. After my master's death, I realized that we had moved into a position of having all the information that was necessary to finally assist humankind in taking control and going after the big prize: immortality. I knew then that my mission was to spread and disseminate this knowledge to every human being, in whatever language, in whatever country.

I have been uncompromising in a mission that I believe can remove chaos from this universe, with the ultimate objective of immortality. The only area in which I have had to make certain concessions has been in the area of the education of my children. Here, my wife Karen and I have realized that we must not jeopardize their access to those establishment facilities critical for their education toward the leadership and administration of the vast and varied programs of the Centre.

Originally, my strategy was one of maintaining a very low profile. Our Centres were to have a very unassuming presence and appearance. In this way, I reasoned, we could quietly focus on our founder's dream of disseminating Kabbalah worldwide. For the first two years after my master's death, the Centre was in a kind of limbo. I did continue the publication programs that he had begun, but I was at a loss for what direction the Kabbalah Centre should take.

All this changed on one fine, fall morning in 1971, two and a half short years after my master had left me. Karen approached me, and said that something had been on her mind for quite some time. Having known Karen for nearly 12 years, I knew that this was not her style. If she had something to say, she usually did not hesitate. Now she suggested that we take a walk in the park. She wanted to discuss something about the future of the Kabbalah Centre. By the time we reached the park, my curiosity had been brewing a while and was fast approaching the boiling point.

"Okay," I said as we began our walk. "Tell me. Spell it out. What's troubling you? Have I done anything wrong?"

"Well," she began, "I know that you are looking for some direction. I know that the Centre has been following the same traditional course for the past 50 years, as all Kabbalists have done over the past two millennia. Despite the efforts of your master and his teacher before him, the ground rules have remained the same. Only students who are rabbis, thoroughly educated in Talmud, over the age of 40 years, have been permitted entry into any of the credible institutions of Kabbalistic teachings, including our own. Your master and his teacher before him have succeeded in removing the veils that had made study of the Kabbalah far too difficult for the uninitiated to undertake. I believe you have to take it from there to another level."

She was trembling slightly. I asked her what she was trying to say.

"What I'm saying…" She paused, tears in her eyes. "What I'm saying is that the time has come for the Centre to open its doors to every man, woman, and child who has a desire to learn."

The very idea made me unsteady on my feet. I found a bench close by and sat down. Karen sat beside me. Open the doors? I thought. Open them to all comers?

"Do you know what you are saying?" I asked Karen. "Are you serious?" I looked across the park, trying to collect my thoughts. Why? Why me? Why now? Where did you get this outlandish thought? I looked at Karen.

"Forget it! It's impossible! It just won't work."

Karen said nothing. She just stared at me like a child caught with her hand in the cookie jar.

I grew silent, too, attempting to collect my thoughts and formulate a response. I had never felt as helpless as I felt at that moment on the park bench next to Karen. After a while, fortunately, I began to regain my composure. I began to meditate, connecting to my master and his teacher. It was then that my master, Rabbi Brandwein, appeared. I gasped and was so frightened that I thought I would faint. Karen stared at me, seeing the look in my eyes. I listened to my master, not saying a word.

"Listen to Karen," he said to me. "Listen to Karen, for she is an incarnation of ------."

I am sorry, dear reader, that for the present I cannot divulge the name I received at that moment. Suffice it to say that my master confirmed that Karen's suggestion of opening the doors to the world was a correct one. It would be a great step toward the elimination of chaos from the landscape of human existence. The work would be difficult. It would pit the entire establishment against us. But, said my master, the antagonism would be coming from a minority establishment since the majority of Jews have left formal religion, as have people in all major religions. My master, like his teacher before him, warned that abandonment of the faith was inevitable if the spiritual aspect was ignored and traditional doctrine prevailed.

This experience in the park ushered in an extraordinary period in our lives. It was beyond our dreams that this decision would affect so many people's lives. We did not realize that our morning walk in the park would unfold as it did.

My immediate response to Karen's suggestion was that we dare not take such a step, despite the message I had received from my master and his teacher. Little did I realize that my negative response would be one of many that I would make upon hearing Karen's revolutionary new ideas. Karen loves to travel the road that has not been traveled before.

Anyone whose upbringing is sheltered finds it difficult to venture outside the protective shield. Karen's life experiences had prepared her for adventure. She was ready for the challenge of change, but I responded negatively, as most people would, until I overcame the programming that had shaped my every decision and action. As I am certain my readers will agree, it is a difficult task to overcome the natural negative response to new ideas.

I knew that if we facilitated open access to Kabbalah, the wrath that would come down upon us might be painful. When I finally realized that this opening was the way, I cautioned Karen that the road we were to embark upon would be lonely. Our friends and family would be uncomfortable with our actions and our lifestyle. In fact, there would be no living person on whom we could rely for help. We would have to find comfort with each other.

THE INTERNATIONAL ROSH HASHANAH EXPERIENCE

The Kabbalistic journey has one main objective,
and that is to restore to humankind a life free from chaos.

So we put out the word that the Centre was going to provide classes for anyone and everyone who wished to learn about Kabbalah. The people began coming. From a handful of the brave, the Centre grew quickly. When we felt that there were enough serious students, we proposed that we attempt a Rosh Hashanah experience according to Kabbalistic teachings. From that small beginning emerged the International Rosh Hashanah experience attended today by about 1,500 people. This experience, which runs a full 54 hours and includes people from all around the globe, leaves participants with the most incredible feeling of spiritual enlightenment and certainty for the entire year.

The Kabbalistic journey enjoyed by its practitioners has one main objective, and that is to restore to humankind a life free from chaos. This is not a dream for the Jews alone. After all, Rosh Hashanah is not an event for Jews alone; this holiday belongs to all of humanity. All people hope for a life filled with joy and fulfillment. People have long searched for this respite from uncertainty and chaos. That is what Rosh Hashanah is all about—to provide humanity with the opportunity of breaking the chains of pain, illness, and suffering. Rosh Hashanah breaks the stranglehold of the Satan over Earth's inhabitants.

THE MOUNT SINAI REVELATION EXPERIENCE

Before my entry into the world of Kabbalah in 1962, I was a traditional, observant Jew. I observed the Jewish holiday known as "Shavuot" in the Orthodox manner. This holiday, which commemorates the giving of the Ten Commandments, required that we study biblical or Talmudic text all night until dawn, at which time we would pray and then go to sleep. This was the way I had observed Shavuot from the age when I was first capable of staying awake all night. As I understood then, it was customary to observe this holiday in commemoration of the event on Mount

Sinai. The reason for studying was to display our connection to the event, and that was all there was to it. It was a traditional observance, with no particular personal meaning for me.

The reader may then imagine how shocked and confused I was when I experienced my first Kabbalistic Shavuot with my master. We seemed to be practicing and observing the holiday just as I had since childhood. It was truly a revelation to me, however, to learn the "why" of the event. This was the explanation of the revelation event and what it was meant to do for me today, 3,400 years later. I could not believe my ears.

My master first reminded me that anyone who referred to this holiday as the commemoration of the giving of the Ten Commandments or the initiation of a new religion, specifically Judaism, was mistaken. Furthermore, he continued, the entire tradition omitted the most significant aspect. When I heard him say this, I was trembling. What had I and all of Jewry throughout the millennia missed? I had been steeped in the religious observance of this event and believed I had been taught all there was to know about the Ten Commandments.

"First," he began, "never again refer to the event as the Lord's Gift of the Ten Commandments. There was no event that signified 'commandments.'"

Upon hearing these words, I might have said, "Good-bye. I really do not want to hear anything more," but my master had a reputation as a rabbi, a scholar, and a Kabbalist, so I stayed. He continued by reciting something I faintly recalled from the Talmud: the statement that what happened on Mount Sinai was the Revelation of the Ten Utterances. Why, I wondered, would the Talmud use the word "utterances?" Most of the world considered the Revelation on Mount Sinai to be the Revelation of the Ten Commandments.

Every movie-goer is familiar with the spectacular movie, <u>The Ten Commandments</u>, directed by Cecil B. DeMille. He literally immortalized the awareness of the revelation incident. Upon learning that the event on Mount Sinai involved not commandments but utterances, however, I asked my master how such a misunderstanding had emerged. Why had this mistaken interpretation been permitted to stretch over millennia?

The answer was shocking. After all my years in rabbinical study, my master's response was a complete deviation as to the methodology used in approaching the more important events of Scriptures. My teacher explained to me that behind every misunderstanding that emerged from the significant event of revelation lay the sinister hand of the Satan, and it was his continued presence that perpetuated this gross distortion. The Satan places great emphasis on maintaining this mistaken interpretation, my master explained. The Satan was familiar with the time of revelation and the ten utterances, but the true purpose of the revelation, said my master, could be summed up in one word: immortality.

Recalling this crucial, new understanding of the connection between Shavuot and immortality, Karen and I decided to establish this long-forgotten tenet that belonged to all of humankind—the Mount Sinai revelation experience. We gave the attendees a mini-experience of immortality by guaranteeing them that by fulfilling the requirements outlined by the Zohar and Rabbi Isaac Luria, they could enjoy the next four months without fear of death. This concept was too much for many, including some who had taken formal classes at the Centre.

Many close friends of the Centre warned us that this guarantee was stretching our luck too far, but Karen and I were determined.

If Kabbalah is indeed the solution and salvation for all humankind, we are going to ride it for all it's worth. The beauty of Kabbalah is that regardless of what one's religion may be, Kabbalistic teachings can rid life of chaos.

THE SATAN CHOOSES KABBALAH AS HIS BATTLEGROUND

The fire of our opponents had been stoked by our success.

Although we had initially begun with a low profile, the momentum behind the Kabbalah Centre adopted a natural, steep curve upward. When the time came to make our presence known to the entire world, our opponents were overwhelmed with what they saw and read. In addition to the very successful Los Angeles Centre, we expanded into Canada, New York, South America, France, and Mexico, everywhere people were hungry for knowledge. The fire of our opponents had been stoked by this success. In their anger, they organized to smear our efforts by whatever means they could find. When it became clear that I was truly bringing Kabbalah to the popular level, the attacks against me were phenomenal. The barrage of criticism and accusations—from the claim that I operated houses of prostitution, to the claim that I owned castles all around the world—was deafening. This Satanic onslaught from the antagonists of Kabbalah has continued to this day.

We knew that this was the Satan's final offensive. Threatened, he took notice of the participants involved in Kabbalah, and what he saw infuriated him. He saw the simple, uneducated, illiterate people learning of the mysteries of Kabbalah. He saw people with no background in Hebrew or Jewish education, and with no connection to anything religious, experiencing the joy and certainty of Kabbalistic teachings. This, he knew, was dangerous. He knew that if this continued, it would bring down his entire kingdom of darkness.

He has fired up his troops with all his energy. The scholars have been behaving irrationally. In addition to their claims that Kabbalah is too holy to touch and too difficult to understand, or that to touch it would bring about insanity, they have woven half-truths and even outright lies into their comments to build the case against Kabbalah.

Their line of attack is now toward those whose mission it is to spread the word of Kabbalah. They are adopting the tactic of discrediting us, of spreading rumors that the people involved in the Centre are brainwashed. All of this, despite Kabbalah's own edict that its teachings must always be subject to careful scrutiny by the student or practitioner.

Pressure mounted against supporters around the world to forsake the Centres and to discontinue their financial support and approval. Friends of our patrons—people who had no idea who we were or what we were all about, who had no knowledge whatsoever of Kabbalah and never visited any Centre nor spoke to any of the administrators—became violent antagonists of Kabbalah and spent much time and effort to dissuade our friends.

This was absolutely the signature of the Satan, for there was no rationale or logic to our opponents' words or behavior. We are certain that the Satan has chosen Kabbalah as his battleground. Since the creation of man, he has never been as threatened as now. But the Light of the Creator, when brought to bear on the Satan, will as easily make him disappear as the flip of a light switch will remove the darkness.

This is what the Light force is prepared to do at any given moment. Just turn more power on, whispers the Light force. You need not concern yourself with fears of chaos and death. You do not need to worry about how to get rid of the scourge of pain and suffering.

Kabbalah teaches us how to turn the Light force on. That's it in a nutshell. Say goodbye to chaos and mortality, and hello to immortality.

THE CONSCIOUSNESS OF SHARING

The idea of loving thy neighbor is not at all dependent upon moral or ethical codes.

An incredible piece of information has been revealed to us by Rabbi Isaac Luria. This information concerns the effects of negative and of positive thinking. When we fill our minds with hatred, envy, and intolerance, our consciousness—which is an energy-intelligence—creates ugly, destructive entities. These entities then implement their awful states of consciousness. There is no question among Kabbalists, however, that the reward for sharing experiences with other people is the creation of positive, protective entities that may be thought of as an expansion, a clone of our life-consciousness-energy.

For this reason, the idea of loving thy neighbor is not at all dependent upon moral or ethical codes. It just doesn't pay to conduct ourselves in any other way. The consequences are too clear. For every negative consciousness manifested, we create a swarm of negative entities that cling to us like bees to honey. They will not release their hold until they have exploited every available sustenance within our bodies and sucked out every drop of Light force.

For those of us who simply want to conduct life's journey with smart logistics, we have no alternative but to behave in a positive manner. This entails never harboring malice toward our fellows. The motivation provided by this understanding is unlike what I had been made to understand all my life before Kabbalah (if I can be considered to have lived before Kabbalah!). I thought only that I should follow the Good Book, the Bible, because that was what God wanted.

This was one of the finest lessons my master taught me. While much of society reveres the Good Book, it has little effect upon our attitudes and behavior toward others. Intolerance has, if anything, increased over the years following the Holocaust of the 1940s. The approach presented by my master achieves the results of the Good Book in a way that is foolproof.

I now comprehend how my master gathered the love of one million people who disagreed with his religious convictions. Everyone who came in contact with my master fell in love with him, just as I did in our first encounter. At first I could not understand what was going on or what was happening—but now I understand.

When we meet people and make friends, we begin to feel an affection for them. This relationship develops to a point where we begin to feel trust. As often as the Satan can have it, however, misunderstandings and disagreements crop up. One thing leads to another until suddenly we find ourselves distant from each other. This situation might well apply to family and relatives, too.

This happens, stated the master, when relationships do not reach a point of unconditional love. Parents, for example, say they love their children. This relationship, however, might have more to do with obligation than with love. This same idea applies to our relationships with friends. We have common interests, and when we want to spend time together, it is because we want the personal benefit of not being alone. This is not unconditional love.

My master, though, had developed the type of sharing that he knew was necessary for his own well-being. He was determined that he would be surrounded constantly with positive entities that would shield and protect him 24 hours a day. My master understood that harboring ill will would summon negative entities. Why invite the enemy?

This was the kind of energy flowing from the master. He had nothing to hide. He wasn't merely putting his best foot forward. My master was anything but charismatic, but anyone who came in contact with him felt this unadulterated, positive energy.

A MESSAGE FOR THE WORLD

"The Satan has no chance when he faces a strong Light."
—*Rabbi Yehuda Brandwein*

One of the most important points repeatedly made when I assumed the leadership of the Centre was that the battering one takes from the Satan will last only as long as weakness is displayed. "The Satan," said my master, "is only as strong as we are weak. The Satan has no chance when he faces a strong Light." When the truth is repeated over and over again, with no hesitation, ultimately the world will accept the truth far more rapidly than the lie. The people who are in the Satan's chaotic employment will always respond to new, imaginative thoughts or concepts, with irrational, outright rejection. The Kabbalist lives by the doctrine "no coercion in spirituality," believing that every person has the freedom of choice to accept or reject the beliefs of others.

LECTURES FOR LAYPEOPLE

The practitioners were always people of sharing.

Religions embrace spiritual teachings that have been neglected and sometimes rejected over the millennia. How, one might ask, were these teachings removed from the established forms of religion? Why weren't the practitioners concerned that these tools become the possession of the people rather than remain the domain of the select few? The answer, of course, is that these same practitioners were not always people of sharing. The revealing of Kabbalah, however, would have to wait until our own day, the so-called 21st century. Now that this millennial time is upon us, the Satan has exerted his greatest effort to combat the spread of these teachings. He understands that when this material becomes available to all, the reality of chaos, pain, and suffering will come to an end. Then, and only then, will the Satan be out of a job.

"Now," my master told me during his appearance in the park that day, "I will reveal for you just exactly what I meant when I told you that support will be forthcoming that you could never imagine. Just as you see me now, you can call upon me when there is a need, and I will be there. There may be questions that I cannot answer sometimes, but understand that my refusal is not my desire or doing. The time of the revelation has not arrived. This may become difficult for you when you are pressed for answers. However, I assure you, my not responding and your frustration as to the lack of an answer or lack of direction will in no way adversely affect you. What is even more surprising is that when you are in doubt as to what course of action or decision you would choose, do not be concerned. Sometimes you may be asked to settle a dispute. Do not be embarrassed to say that you do not know how to resolve the matter if indeed you are in doubt. When in doubt, do nothing. Merely respond that you have not received your response. More often than not, those who are not very close to you may not understand your response. Do not fret or become irritated by their lack of understanding. This is a cardinal and essential rule. You are never to experience the ego when you answer or say 'I do not know.' You will come to understand, although it is a difficult lesson, that the rational, conscious mind is nothing more than a blip on the physical-reality level of existence. You have been programmed to accept the rational mind as the only faculty with which you can decide, organize, relate to others, and, above all, think. This notion came about completely and painlessly through the Satan and his influence."

WE ARE NOT IN CONTROL

The rational mind never controls more than four to six percent of our activities.

This is exactly the way the Satan has manipulated humankind. The Satan has influenced us into believing that with a proper and skillful mind, we are in control, and we actually believe it even when we lose control and chaos enters our lives. We'll find every conceivable reason why things went wrong. However, the real reason, which is, "I am not in control," is avoided at all costs. That is exactly the awesome and disguised power of the Satan—never to let on that he is behind our inability to maintain control over our lives. The rational mind never controls more than four to six percent of our activities, whether in speech, hearing, or sight. How many of us consciously think or consciously speak each and every word that comes out of our mouths? Unless a speaker is delivering a prepared text, it is undoubtedly clear that he or she is unaware of each word emanating from the mouth. Where did the structure of each sentence come from? If not from some invisible prepared script, it is not and cannot be from the rational mind, for the rational mind is not thinking or conscious of what is being said. The same holds true of any chit-chat between two friends. "Consequently," stated my master, "as of this moment on, you are to prepare lectures for lay-men (thousands of lectures) to be given in the Centres all around the world."

"But," I protested, "I haven't had any experience or reason to create lectures, other than possibly a few sermons in the past. You are now suggesting that I sit down, do the research, prepare a presentation for the layman so he understands these very difficult concepts in layman's language—and thousands of lectures, at that. This is undoubtedly a project for many years, assuming I even had forty-eight hours in the day. And with all the difficulties that this assignment includes, the project will also include, aside from Kabbalistic text, discussions of reincarnation, astrology, medita-tion, the power of the Aleph-Bet, biology, and other subjects. Then, of course, when students have taken all the beginner's courses, I guess I'm to construct advanced courses as well."

"If you are somewhat confused," said my master, "I cannot blame you. If I were you, I would be more than confused. I would be dumbfounded. Inasmuch as you comprehend the inadequacy of the rational mind, you will now be prepared for what I have to reveal to you. I have on many occasions spoken to you about how Rabbi Ashlag came to write tens of thousands of pages on so difficult a subject as Kabbalah. One might have suspected that these works would take many lifetimes and certainly not be completed within some thirty years—and this in addition to his other duties that took away many hours a day of writing time."

If you recall, I mentioned that my teacher stated that he wrote nothing. Thus I once asked Rabbi Ashlag, "If you did not write all these pages, who did?"

His reply was, "The pen."

Rabbi Ashlag explained this new phenomenon by saying that he now connected to the 94 or 96 percent of the true consciousness or mind. Consequently, the pen was merely taking all the information that had been waiting in the wings for millennia and putting it down on paper. The large volume of material was in fact not his. He was merely a good stenographer who permitted the totality of the mind to come through without interference from the Satan's rational-mind consciousness, which says not to believe anything unless you can see it. This is the greatest hoax with which the Satan has afflicted humankind. But the Satan could not, and did not, dominate the mind of Rabbi Ashlag.

To make matters more confusing, Rabbi Ashlag's teacher taught him all he knew in a matter of six months. Now how could his teacher reveal to Rabbi Ashlag all the information that ever was, is, and will be in a matter of six short months? This and many other mysteries that we may have to grapple with originate within the rational mind-consciousness. A man-made calculator can multiply many numbers, and yet our rational minds have difficulty doing the same job in considerably more time.

My master told me, "Therefore, I will continue to teach you as I have prior to 1969. I am now capable of revealing to you that which was impossible while I was, figuratively speaking, alive. I am very much alive for you now, and your pen will begin to write for you. Not only will you experience an incredible number of lectures, which your pen shall set down on paper, but you will no longer have to prepare for seminars and conferences. Just ask me to be there with you. Just know the topic and a rough outline of what you want to talk about. Leave the rest to me."

"In addition, prepare to write books, and I will assist you in choosing the topics for the volumes you produce. And do not worry about the money necessary for their printing. It will always be there. Furthermore, do not be overly concerned or devote too much time in search of printers. They will always appear at the right time. And that is about all that we are to discuss for the time being. So begin immediately with your mission."

Needless to say, I was beside myself. I was convinced that I was hallucinating. How else could I explain meeting up with my master after an absence of two years? How could I explain the conversation that seemed to have been going on between us? I certainly wished it to be true, but it was too good to be true. My experience within the world of Kabbalah, however, had taught me never to outright reject any idea that can enhance our lives, and so, with the guidance of the master, Karen and I embarked on a new stage in the wonderful world of Kabbalah.

Many of you undoubtedly assume that anyone who goes through an experience such as mine must be gullible, vulnerable to unconventional and paranormal phenomena. Having spent seven years in an inseparable relationship with my master, I was conditioned to grasp the very heartbeat of this individual. We were truly one soul. I never felt that my master was outside of my self. Only someone who has experienced a similar relationship can understand what we felt. It was like the return of a loved one who has been absent for a few weeks. Upon my master's return, I felt as if I were complete again. There was no room or any empty space for questions. I was just happy that we were reunited.

THE MISSION OF REMOVING CHAOS FROM THE UNIVERSE

Of course, the intent of this book is not to answer all questions that can be raised. There are many other works by this author that address a great many other questions. This book is intended to deal with one subject: immortality.

Let us now return to the matter of revelation. What seems to emerge from the Zohar's interpretation is that revelation is about the Light force becoming fully manifested and revealed. The instrument by which the revelation came to fruition, and brought to an end to the chaos and mortality that had afflicted humankind since the sin of Adam, is the Torah. This was a dramatic moment in the history of civilization. Death and chaos were swept from the human landscape.

The full radiance and beneficence of the Light

force permeated every nook and cranny of the cosmos. There was no room left for darkness. Immortality had been restored to its place within the world community. Therefore, to assume that revelation is only intended for the Jews is a mistake. The benefits accrued to all living beings, as well as to inanimate objects. Clothing and similar items were no longer subject to the laws of entropy. The miracle of revelation, the miracle that enabled the Jews to possess clothing that never wore away, was just that—a miracle.

Moses, as a direct result of his connection with certainty consciousness and the Light force, never severed his relationship with the Tree of Life reality. This affinity and bond is what prompted the Zohar to remark, "Moses never died." This matter will be more fully explored later on. The awesome power of Moses that is described in Scriptures, came as no surprise to Kabbalists. In my early years in Kabbalah, however, this statement about Moses was incomprehensible, even when told to me by my master, but this is the way of Kabbalist. When revealing information that disturbs people, recall what the Nazis maintained: "Repeat the lie one thousand times, and the world shall accept it as truth."

"When you believe that something is true and can benefit humankind," remarked my master, "then you must have the courage to withstand the onslaught of negative, unfounded criticism. Just because no one has heard your remarks before, or the information has not come into the public domain, do not falter. Be prepared to accept the abuse and nasty remarks that will inevitably come your way."

THE THEME IS UNIVERSAL

Behind every evil act of humankind
stood the armada of the Satan.

"I know," he continued, "that this kind of explanation and interpretation is a complete departure from what you, and conventional Judaism along with all other established religions, have been assuming as to this great, memorable event in history." He paused. "It is radical and revolutionary," my master went on, "and be prepared for the time in the very near future when you will be called upon to deliver to the entire world this timely message."

But what was more jolting, and yet revealing, was this new concept, stating that behind every evil act of humankind stood the armada of the Satan. As I have mentioned, adherents of all religions believed that any act or event that embraced the forces of evil was a manifestation of God's wrath upon the sinners. The tragic inclusion of good, honest people within the Holocaust trauma was a personal matter of the Lord, one that we had no right to question. This my master completely rejected, and he went further to quote the universal rule of holocaust: when the Satan has been given permission to unleash his violence upon humankind, he sweeps whole areas without discrimination. To anyone in his path who does not learn the secrets of how to create a shield around himself, another universal law applies: "Ignorance of the law is no excuse."

The recent Holocaust, while bringing down the wrath of the Satan upon 6 million Jews, at the same time saw the Satan's evil hand of destruction and death swallow up millions of people of other religions and nationalities. The culprit in this awful massacre was the originator of death and violence: the Satan. "Then what was the truthful, Kabbalistic interpretation of the revelation event," I asked, "if not to provide humankind with some moral and ethical guidelines?"

"The idea of forming a religious cult was the furthest idea from the Lord's mind," said my master. "The theme is universal, despite what traditionally we have been taught or led to believe."

What did my master mean, I wondered, when he said the theme was universal?

My master then threw the ball into my court. "Don't you remember that the Talmud specifically made much of the fact that the entire Decalogue was translated into every language? So that every nation would participate in its revelations?"

"Yes," I replied. However, I did not understand the point my master was making. "So the Lord wanted all nations to be aware of what the Jewish people were receiving," I said. "What is so unusual about that?"

"You still do not understand the revelation aspect of Mount Sinai," my master said. "You remain with your programmed education." He became a little impatient with my delay in grasping the point. "Revelation was not about the ten utterances, but rather, the revealing of the total embodiment of the Light force in our universe—complete and universal communion with the Light, which left no area or place where darkness could conceal itself. The result was the demise of death, which had ruled and affected all Creation, including man, since the sin of Adam. The world had achieved the most sought-after gift humankind could ever have longed and hoped for—Immortality".

Then what was the Decalogue or Ten Utterances about, now that I had discarded the remnants of a corrupted Ten Commandments?

"The Ten Utterances," stated my master, "were nothing more than the instrument by which the immaterial Light force of the Lord became physically expressed in our universe. They were no different than a light bulb that reveals electric current or, for that matter, the physical body that reveals and makes manifest the immaterial, internal soul."

THE HEBREW LETTERS

The Hebrew letters were no ordinary letters.

The Hebrew letters of the Ten Utterances and words and verses made up of these letters, were nothing more than a vehicle whereby the full impact of the Light force made its presence known and felt in the universe. This was specifically directed toward the Satan's law of chaos and mortality. The Hebrew letters were no ordinary letters. They were the building blocks or blueprints for the expression of the Light force. I understand this today as analogous to the microscopic DNA, which channels the life force of an individual.

"The Hebrew letters were the building blocks of the entire universe," continued my master, citing a 4,000-year-old Kabbalistic book with which I was unfamiliar. I was dumbfounded. Is this what the Hebrew letters were all about?

To the best of my knowledge, the Hebrew language was just that—a language for the Hebrews.

However, when I was confronted with The Book of Formation, written by Avraham the Patriarch, who lived around 2000 B.C.E., I immediately realized that this work existed almost 300 or 400 years before the revelation of the Ten Utterances. Of course, I said to myself, this language existed long before there were Jews.

"Furthermore," continued my master, "the Zohar, infers from the Biblical text that prior to the Tower of Babel incident, the universal language of humanity was Hebrew."

I then remembered that Christopher Columbus brought with him an interpreter in order to speak with as-yet-undiscovered people, and that this interpreter spoke Hebrew. I also remembered that when the forefathers of the United States were considering breaking away from British rule, they wanted to sever their ties so completely that they preferred to no longer speak English. One of the languages considered was Hebrew. Yet today, most people, including myself, think of the Hebrew language as Jewish.

SECTION II

THE STRUGGLE BETWEEN THE DARKNESS AND THE LIGHT

"GOD SAID 'LET THERE BE LIGHT;'
AND THERE WAS LIGHT.
GOD SAW THAT THE LIGHT WAS GOOD,
AND GOD SEPARATED THE LIGHT
FROM THE DARKNESS."

CONTROL THROUGH KABBALAH

"Patience is a virtue that you must acquire as rapidly as possible."
—*Rabbi Yehuda Brandwein*

Undoubtedly, you, the reader, have been questioning much of what has been written here. Fortunately,
as I have indicated, to study Kabbalah is to question
over and over. I questioned my master many times,
and always his reply was accompanied by a warm and
gentle smile. Finally he felt that I fully understood the
basic concepts and, more importantly, the answers to
the many "Why?" questions I had asked him. He
explained to me that simply understanding these
things would "set the process in motion." Without this
understanding, he explained, time would simply pass
by, as it has for so many millennia, and nothing would
change. "Patience is a virtue that you must acquire as
rapidly as possible," he told me. "Sooner or later the
Satan will meet you head-on, a reminder that nothing
has as yet happened. We are in a quantum era where
infinite components must come together and fit as
one unified whole. You have laid the groundwork, you
have completed the preliminary work. But always
remember, all of the parts must be assembled when the
moment for transformation presents itself."

This was a valuable lesson, one that would stand
me in good stead when I became impatient—and it is
easy to become impatient, for although you need

only turn on the Light, the Satan is still undefeated. The struggle between the darkness and the Light continues.

THE REVELATION OF THE TEN UTTERANCES

What is new is the coming together at last of science and religion.

The understanding of the true significance of what occurred on Mount Sinai is of great import. Once you turn on this understanding, it increases in brightness, and more and more of the true meaning of this event is revealed. In order for the process of mortality to be reversed, every single one of the components must be prepared in order to realize the whole. Additionally, the process must occur in harmony with the cosmic calendar. Only in this way can the energy for immortality be released at the appropriate time, with the right consciousness. Each and every year the right moment comes around. This is the significance of revelation.

Again, the image of the electric bulb is of use to us. In order for electrical energy to be utilized, there must be an electrical bulb to contain the electrical energy. The moment the electrical current is held within the bulb, the energy will be revealed. This is the paradoxical nature of our universe. In order for our soul to be revealed, it is must be held within the body.

This concept is very similar to the idea of atomic energy—an energy so great that before it had been released, it literally could not be imagined. The energy of the atom is held within the atom, but if we split that atom, the energy is released and we are able to use it.

The idea of immortality is familiar to people of many religions. It is nothing new. What is new is the coming together at last of science and religion, the assembling of all of the components that previously had been polarized at opposite sides of a great chasm in which humanity longed for wholeness, but was kept in the dark.

Yes, the immortality energy is present within the Light. With the right meditations and the complete wisdom of Kabbalah, people are allowed to tap into the Light's awesome energy, drawing it into their bodies. Meeting its enemy, mortality energy, the Light force is capable of completely eliminating mortality, as if it had never been there, just as a light bulb eliminates darkness from a room when the switch is turned on.

KABBALAH SWEEPS CHAOS AWAY

That's the way the Satan has our minds going,
back and forth, back and forth...

Although we now have unprecedented command over material reality, as science frequently reminds us, the Satan often unsettles our minds and we forget this sense of control. How rapidly we are overwhelmed by chaos! Have you ever watched a game of Ping-Pong in full swing and noticed the heads of people as they observe the ball dashing from one player to another? That's the way the Satan has our minds going—back and forth, back and forth, from chaos to an all-too-tenuous sense of control.

The Zohar states that humankind unquestionably has the ability to dominate all of physical reality and to remove the interference that is presented by this reality. Remember that the rational, conscious mind is nothing more than an interference, and the Satan distracts us by having us watching our thoughts dart chaotically back and forth.

The "miracles" we are familiar with are demonstrations of powers we have access to through Kabbalah. When the Red Sea interfered with the flight of the Israelites from Egypt, they could have focused on their rational mind, which told them that if they continued into the sea they would drown. Yet they were able to split the Red Sea because humankind is part of God and therefore has the divine ability to achieve such "miraculous events." The Israelites did not allow themselves to be dissuaded by the waves they saw with their eyes, because they entered into the separate reality of the mind and into God.

How was it that the Israelites forgot this ability? How, after witnessing this miracle, could they ever hesitate again?

The Zohar explains this: Just as revelation displayed the power of one moment, the Satan also seizes the moment, and the separation of mind and physical reality are forgotten.

The body is material; the mind is non-material. It is through the bridge of Kabbalah's secret codes, which includes a powerful tool known as the 72 Names, that the mind can be brought to bear upon the material world.

Explaining the 72 Names and other aspects and tools of Kabbalah is not the task that is now before me. It is not necessary, however, to know all these things in order to understand the simple power of Kabbalah that it is my task to present. Just as we do not need to understand all the secrets of the genetic code in order to carry these genes forward, so the power of

Kabbalah has its own integrity and life. We have only to enter into it; it is already within us.

THE UNDIFFERENTIATED AND THE DIFFERENTIATED STATES

The Satan has no affinity for an undifferentiated state.

There exists only one source of energy: the Light of the Creator. How the energy is put to use is left to humankind. It might be used for productive purposes or for malicious purposes. Fundamentally, the Light force brings rewards to humankind. However, when the Satan gains access to any form of existence—whether it be human, animal, vegetable, or inanimate—he has the opportunity to make use of the Light force.

Fully aware of the threat to all of His creation, the Creator devised a plan whereby the Satan could not bring about unrestricted chaos. The plan, my master told me, was that every entity would undergo death and rebirth. Death would mean that the Light force would completely withdraw and would disappear when a new physical cell or any other vessel reappeared. After the cells had completed their development, which scientists estimate takes approximately seven years, the Light withdraws and the Satan "leaves go." When the Satan's appetite (the desire to receive for the self alone) cannot be fulfilled, he exits.

Through this procedure, the cells are free to return to their undifferentiated state of existence. At this level of being, they are subject to an attachment with the Satan, but the Satan has no affinity for an undifferentiated state, and therefore, he cannot bond with the cell.

In my master's words, "When the cell reaches the point of becoming a lung or a heart—the so-called 'differentiated state,' the Satan and his armada of negative entities can then link up with the cell. When the cell is still in an undifferentiated potential state of existence, the Satan does not have the capability to bond with the cell. In a potential state, the cell is beyond the grasp of negative entities."

The Satan and all bearers of chaos, although fed by the Light of the Creator, receive only a limited infusion of it—just enough to remain alive. Only when they have penetrated the protective coating of a cell are the Satan and his helpers sufficiently charged to devour the cell's energy. Once they have made contact with the DNA, the Light force must withdraw. Once the Satan has gained access, the entire body is his domain."

THE INVASION POINTS
OF THE SATAN

Negative activity allows the Satan access.

"But what has caused these openings that allow the Satan access?" I asked my master.

"Negative activity," he responded. "When an action with conscious thought affects another human being negatively, or when a violation of basic good principles has come to pass, then the person who is responsible for this negativity increases his quantity of 'negative entities.' That person alone created those entities. The natural protective shield becomes vulnerable to these newly created negative entities."

Ever the questioner, I asked, "But why can't the natural protective shield keep out these newly formed entities, as it keeps the Satan at bay? Just as a newborn child has bacteria all around and its protective shield thwarts these energies from causing harm, why can't a person's negative entities still remain harmless?"

Here my master reminded me of a conversation in which he had stated that because these negative entities were of the individual's own making, they had greater access. The protective shield permitted their entry. Once the door opened, it was kept open to permit other negative entities—including those not of the individual's own creation—to enter.

THE PROTECTIVE SHIELD

Following its final stage of development, the cell normally remains with the Light force DNA intact. As nature would have it, however, at that point, the Light force DNA, having fulfilled its mission to bring about the finished product, withdraws. It is a complete cycle, for the Satan departs as well, and the cell can return to the undifferentiated state to once again start the seven-year cycle all over again.

My master explained to me that when there is an ongoing active stage where the cell is differentiating toward its final state, the protective shield remains active. However, once the final stage of the process has been reached, then the protective shield has no purpose. Differentiation has been achieved. Paradoxically, the Satan can then invade the cell.

THE SATAN'S FORMIDABLE ENEMY: THE LIGHT

Positive thought produces positive activity and gives us control of our destiny.

Returning to our consideration of the Israelites, we can firmly state that the Israelites and all human beings are God. Yet there is one distinction between God Himself and human beings. Whereas a person has a body, God does not. It is the human body that creates a particular liability: a sense of fragmentation—that is, the separation of individual consciousness. To overcome this liability, people are provided with certain methods by which the God-like feature within us is brought to bear on the physical reality.

Although the 3,400 years that people have lived under the heel of the Satan is only a moment within the infinity of time that immortality represents, naturally, in our mortal life, it appears impressive. So when both physicists and Kabbalists developed theories that stress that the only reality is consciousness, sometimes they have trouble accepting their own theories.

These theories must be taken seriously. We should not run from the truth merely because our rational minds cannot presently fathom it. The secret lies in dismissing the thoughts that whisper in our ears, "Oh, this is just too far out. It can't be." These thoughts are the work of the Satan. Know your enemy—the Satan—and you are set free. It's as easy as that.

There is only one foe out there: the Satan. I know that these words sound strange, but shortly this will become music as sweet as any, and it will bring us tranquillity and contentment.

But if the Satan is our only enemy, what are we to think about those who come dressed in bodies? Those who at this moment do not share our knowledge of

Kabbalah, our knowledge of the Light? Are they strange demons? No, they are real people, with consciousness just like ours.

If we are positive in every way, no enemy of any kind can bring harm to us. Just as the darkness in a room cannot wage war with the light, the Satan gets to us only if we open ourselves to his negativity. Positive thought produces positive activity and gives us control of our destiny.

DESIRE TO RECEIVE FOR THE SELF ALONE BECOMES DESIRE TO RECEIVE FOR THE SAKE OF SHARING

"The Zohar places a great deal of emphasis upon the awesome power of thought."
—*Rabbi Yehuda Brandwein*

Positive thought has such power because the universe is itself an enormous composite of thought. This is true also for all human beings in the universe. All that exists is thought, from a dinner table or a home, to an electromagnetic energy field. Like the Light force, in whose image we were created, the consciousness of our minds is not only where information is stored; it is where energy and knowledge are created.

"At a table in a restaurant where we may choose to sit," explained my master, "the former occupants have instilled their thought consciousness, which may be positive or negative. When we rent or purchase a new home, we must recognize that the thought consciousness of its previous residents is permeating the house. Were they positive or negative people?"

When we recall Sir James Jeans, who also stated that thought is the only reality, we realize that the Kabbalist is in complete agreement with him, with one further consideration. For the Kabbalist, reality is not considered to encompass only outer space or the universe at large. It was my master's deep discovery that applied this truth to the personal level. The material world, the world of matter, as opposed to the world of thought, is where chaos creeps in. At the personal level, it is the physical body that interferes with our thought processes, often by obscuring them.

This interference takes the form of what my master called the desire to receive for the self alone—this is the energy-intelligence of the body. In contrast, the Light energy-intelligence of the spirit is called the desire to receive for the sake of sharing.

Kabbalistic teachings are a way of life. They are neither a religion nor a philosophy. "These teachings are by no means effortless," remarked my master. "The right cultivation of the desire to receive for the sake of sharing is very demanding. No pain, no gain.

The Zohar places a great deal of emphasis upon the awesome power of thought, to the extent that inanimate objects, like the Tablets on Mount Sinai, are also subject to our thought consciousness. Misfortune and illness are never separate or apart from our thoughts. Our mind and body, our thought and environment, are inseparable. Therefore, not just the disease or problem must be treated, but the thoughts of the self and the thoughts of others. Our state of mind can make us and others well and can speed recovery from illness. We have the power to heal and the power to remain well. We also have the power to bring our bodies, and all material things, to immortality."

USE OF THE LIGHT FORCE

With the dawning of the 21st century,
Kabbalah is going to come into its own.

Even in the days of Moses, DNA existed. Although it would be another 3,400 years before it would be discovered, the famous "double helix" shape of this basic genetic material was present, directing the formulation of every living thing, from algae to human beings.

Now, in our own day, scientists are attempting to redirect or alter the DNA codes where flaws or deficiencies exist. The methodology of Kabbalah may be thought of as the genetic re-engineering of the future,

101

in which the mind and consciousness, rather than the scalpel or laser, will play the major role.

Just as a software program must be working correctly to enable a computer to function, the proper circuitry of DNA must be in place to animate living beings. From Kabbalistic perspective, it is easy to imagine taking various physical functions—those of the heart and lung and limb—and returning them to their undifferentiated state. By returning the damaged cells of the organ to the "repair shop," the cells may be restored to their original state of good health and may then return to their point of designation, whether it be the heart, lung, or limb.

The concept is not an easy one for the rational mind to accept, but in the realm of high technology, nothing can be written off as "myth." So it perhaps becomes easier to understand that appropriate use of the Light force constitutes a prime example of mind over matter. And with the dawning of the 21st century, Kabbalah is going to come into its own. As the collective consciousness of the human race is raised—an inevitable event, with the widespread influence of Kabbalah—science will come to realize that it is possible to eliminate a physical entity or material expression, such as a cancerous tumor, by rolling it back to its original, embryonic, undifferentiated state. Indeed, in our lifetime, laypeople will achieve flawless health and fly around the globe using nothing more (and nothing less!) than consciousness.

KABBALAH AS TOTAL EMBODIMENT OF THE LIGHT FORCE

When our consciousness is elevated, we can recognize the body for what it really is: a vehicle for Light force soul expression.

The Light force comprises 99 percent of all physical entities. When the Light force becomes assertive, the material becomes differentiated and is dominated by the Light force. It is precisely for this reason that tumors can be diminished. Tumors and other bodily interferences are from the dark side. They are no longer assertive when the Light force has been activated, just as the darkness disappears when the light goes on in a room.

When our consciousness is elevated, we can recognize the body for what it really is—a vehicle for Light force-soul expression. Then the physical body no longer dominates the Light force–soul. The body no longer can place its limitations on the Light force-soul. One phenomenon made possible by this fact, that is soon to be revealed, is the ability of the human being to fly just like a bird around the globe. Envisioned by the Zohar 3,400 years ago, such a situation will no longer remain outside the realm of the possible.

This capacity for flight is already being demonstrated in outer space, where a person can travel around a globe of 24,000 miles in less than one hour. Both Rabbi Shimon, author of the Zohar, and Rabbi Isaac Luria, the Ari, could travel great distances in a matter of minutes. The secret lies in the ability to control the interference of gravity and friction.

The weight of a slab of stone is measured in physical terms. If the interference, or limiting feature, of stone was removed by our consciousness, however, then the 99 percent Light force would dominate the stone reality. The only reason humans cannot carry weight ten times their own is simply that they are programmed to accept heavy weight as a legitimate interference. Our consciousness decides that the interference is too great, and we announce, "This weight is too heavy to lift."

THE BIBLE AS THE ROAD MAP OF LIFE'S JOURNEY

The question precedes the answer.

This must have been the way the Israelites felt, with the Egyptians in hot pursuit, when they came to the Red Sea. They began to pray to God. "Save us!" they shouted to God. What do you think was God's reply? "Why are you shrieking to me?"

I've read that verse in the Bible possibly a thousand times, and as a Kabbalist, I asked "Why?" What kind of response was this from a loving, compassionate God? In time of need, to whom should one pray, if not to the Lord? Was the Lord so heartless that He refused to heed their pleas?

The Biblical verse just noted includes an even more baffling suggestion by the Lord. He told the Israelites that they should jump into the sea.

What do you think the Israelites thought when they heard these words? "You're a big help, God. Why do I need enemies when I have friends like you?"

We must ask a major question here. If God provided, in this crucial instance, so little solace, where did the whole idea of prayer come from? All religions include prayer as the most significant aspect of religious participation.

Yet, the fact that they do is just another example of how our minds have ceased to function inquisitively. Kabbalist warns that failing to question will shut down the possibility of receiving an answer. The truth of the matter is that we have simply been programmed into the acceptance of prayer. Rather than praying, we must question. The question precedes the answer.

Could this be one of the reasons that the Bible has lost so many of its readers? I'm certain that most people who read the verse discussed here are confused by it, possibly even angered by it. We cannot, however, simply dismiss the verse as incomprehensible. The Zohar, that wellspring of knowledge and information, comes to the rescue. The Zohar understands that the Bible is a coded text. When decoded, it will return to its rightful position as the road map of life's journey.

While Moses was present, he could keep the Israelites in line, constantly reminding them that they need not resort to prayers, need not plead to God for assistance. The Bible tells us how the Red Sea was split: it was split by the Israelites holding the reality of it splitting in their minds. Mind over matter! This is the true message of this passage. Yet, as was customary with the Israelites, they forgot this message all too quickly.

KABBALAH AS THE BATTLEGROUND OF THE SATAN

Satan's building block is the ego.

To address this verse, the Zohar faces all these difficulties, and others as well. What this incredible verse is attempting to reveal, states the Zohar, is the power given to these chosen Israelites in the final removal of all limitations placed upon us by physical reality. No longer can these limitations have an effect upon us.

This concept is revolutionary, and I see clearly the hand of the Satan reaching out to the readers of this book, appealing to each reader's present level of consciousness, saying "Come on! You don't believe any of this. Surely there is the idea of mind over matter, but the power of the mind cannot eliminate a cancerous tumor! Has it been done?"

These are the famous last words of the Satan. The Satan's building block is the ego, one of his most powerful tools in creating fragmentation between people. All people with large egos see themselves as better than the next person.

What a surprise that it is the scientists who have appeared to proclaim that consciousness and mind are all there is. The physical, material reality of our existence is secondary to our minds.

It is only when we really identify my master trickster behind chaos—the Satan—that we can defend ourselves properly against his assault on our consciousness. The tools to make this defense invincible and lasting will become available for all to use. We shall then approach the state of existence that prevailed during the time of the master, Kabbalist Rabbi Shimon bar Yochai.

THE PLEA OF THE SATAN

The Satan once approached God and pleaded that He ask Rabbi Shimon to leave the physical world and make sure that his presence would no longer be recognized or felt by other humans. His plea ran as follows: "I have used every possible means at my disposal to bring chaos into the life of Rabbi Shimon and all peoples. Rabbi Shimon has thwarted and resisted my every effort toward this end. But now he has turned his efforts to counteroffensive, seeking me out wherever I am, even when I am not on a rampage against humanity. He successfully hones in on his target and miraculously seeks out and destroys anything in his path that I empower with chaos and devastation. My mission within the scheme of Creation no longer is viable nor purposeful! I cannot exert the desire to receive for oneself alone! If evil is banished from the consciousness of humanity by virtue of my inability to influence people, then their free will to choose between good and evil will disappear. People will no longer need to make any effort to overcome evil instincts and will opt for a positive consciousness. The consciousness of hate, ego, and self-indulgence, the root of all evil, will go out of existence. Consequently, Rabbi Shimon must be asked to leave this mortal earthly existence so that I can ply my trade of evil consciousness."

AND THE POWERS OF THE SATAN MUST NOT BE UNDERESTIMATED

Rabbi Shimon left behind the legacy of the Zohar.

It was thus that Rabbi Shimon chose to leave behind our familiar landscape, which had undergone temporary rehabilitation. Pain and suffering had no place while Rabbi Shimon was among the living. Of course, few individuals were cognizant of this unique person's effect. Most people assumed that they were just lucky to live in this period. Such is the case with many of us today who feel "lucky" when we escape the apparent chaos that overtakes our friends and families.

When Rabbi Shimon left the world, however, people were left in a far better position than when he first made his entrance. He left the world a legacy, the ultimate weapon by which humankind will bring down the empire of doom and chaos. That testimonial is his Zohar.

THE BIBLE AS A CODED INSTRUMENT

"The Bible is nothing more than a coded instrument to reach the essential understanding of how mortality came into existence."
—*Rabbi Yehuda Brandwein*

Well, how can chaos rule the day when the Zohar is among us?

We have only to go back to the story of Adam and Eve to answer this question. How can chaos rule the day when the wonderful reality described in Genesis is with us? This reality does not include the flaws and chaos of the physical, material world.

"Do I understand correctly," I asked my master, "that mortality began when Adam ate from the Tree of Knowledge?"

"Yes," my master replied. "However, the Bible is nothing more than a coded instrument to reach the essential understanding of how mortality came into existence."

Why, asks the Kabbalist, did the Lord prohibit Adam and Eve from eating the fruit of the Tree of Knowledge and, at the same time, warn them that if they did eat it they would become subject to mortality and would surely die? Was the Tree of Knowledge a tree of poison?

When the snake convinced Eve to eat the forbidden fruit, it assured her she would not die. Adam and Eve did not die after eating from the Tree of Knowledge. God warned them that eating the forbidden fruit would result in their death, while the snake told Adam and Eve that they would not die.

Are we to assume that the snake knew something that God did not? Does the Bible imply that God sometimes makes mistakes? Or could God have been outsmarted by the snake? What did God mean when he told Adam that if they ate from the fruit of the Tree of Knowledge they would die?

The answers are simple, but profound. The entire section of the Bible about the forbidden fruit refers to nothing less than consciousness itself.

HOW PURE CONSCIOUSNESS IS CORRUPTED BY THE MASTER MAGICIAN, THE SATAN

Adam and Eve were nothing more than pure consciousness.

The Tree of Knowledge and its fruits of Good and Evil refer to how pure consciousness is corrupted by the master magician, the Satan. Before eating the fruit, Adam and Eve knew only pure consciousness. There was no limitation, fragmentation, or mortality. They knew that life consisted of eternity. Endings, decay, and chaos were all illusions.

When they partook of the forbidden fruit, however, they connected with the illusionary realm of limitation, fragmentation, and death consciousness, with the origin of all the chaos and decay so familiar to the world we know today. Their previous level of pure consciousness was touched by the Satan.

At the beginning of the Bible, there is no mention of the Tree of Life or the Tree of Knowledge, because at that time physical existence, as we know it, had not come into being. Adam and Eve were nothing more than pure consciousness. This is, of course, difficult to grasp. Today, when so much emphasis is placed on a body being fit and beautiful, who has time to think about the more important aspects of ourselves, such as our thoughts, our consciousness?

However, despite the glorification of the body, we are aware of the deeper qualities of people—their character, how they think, their consciousness.

THE SATAN'S NEED
FOR PHYSICAL REALITY

The Satan needed physical reality
in order to set up his kingdom of chaos and death.

The Bible teaches us that originally there was no physical body, and the Satan could not connect with pure consciousness and corrupt it. When the physical realm came into being, however, the Satan had the opportunity to become attached to our consciousness through our physical bodies. Corrupt, limited, fragmented consciousness could then take control. Whether the Satan would be successful in his quest to reign over humankind was left to Adam and Eve in accordance with the doctrine of free will.

Before the coexistence of consciousness and body, the Tree of Life and the Tree of Knowledge could not serve as a means for the Satan to make contact with the essence of a human being. The Satan needed physical reality in order to set up his kingdom of chaos and death. Before the Satan could go to work, Adam and Eve had to have a consciousness of death and chaos.

When Adam and Eve ate the forbidden fruit, their previously pure Tree of Life consciousness was defiled by exposure to the Satan's chaotic consciousness. The Tree of Life became subject to the limitations and illusions of the Tree of Knowledge.

God knew that upon connecting with the fruit, Adam would be vulnerable. God knew that Adam would become subject to the illusionary realm of death, and that did not necessarily mean that Adam and Eve were to die immediately after eating the fruit.

Young people believe they will live forever. As

adults, we know that a weekend drive in the country could kill us. However, we think, statistics on traffic fatalities are really for others. When we return home safe and sound from our weekend drive, we feel confident that we have outsmarted death. When the snake said to Adam and Eve, "Eat the fruit," he might just as well have said, "Take a ride in your car, and you'll see that you're smarter than God." That's exactly what convinced Adam and Eve. They were trying to outsmart death.

WHAT GOD TOLD ADAM AND EVE

"Your previous consciousness of immortality will die…" This is what God told Adam and Eve: "When the Satan said that although you eat from the fruit you will not die, he meant that you will not die right now. But your previous consciousness of immortality will die right away. The Satan has promised you only a temporary reprieve from death. Furthermore, when you die, you shall leave a legacy of death consciousness that shall prevail until what will be called the twenty-first century. After you die—and assuredly you shall one day die—only then will you understand what those living in that time will learn about immortality, which you will know again only after you die."

And this is where we are now, in the new millennium, when the master magician, the Satan, will at last be exposed as the master trickster. Mortality is illusionary. Immortality is real.

THE SATAN'S ACCESS TO THE LIGHT FORCE

Becoming embodied within the physical realm opened things up to the Satan.

As we have indicated, a major Kabbalistic principle is that the Light force cannot express itself unless it becomes concealed in a physical vessel. My master's instruction for understanding this is to imagine electrical current, an example that works so beautifully that I will reiterate it here.

Since an electrical current is non-material, it requires containment within a physical object for it to become revealed and manifested. Similarly, the soul, without a body, remains invisible and unnoticed. So the Light force must become encased if it is to share its beneficence.

Becoming embodied within the physical realm, however, opened things up to the Satan. As long as the Light force had remained divorced from the physical realm, there had been no danger. Now the Satan could be nourished by the Light force, just as a parasite is nourished. The physical realm gave the Satan the extra strength required to create global and internal chaos.

THE SOUL'S STRUGGLE WITH REALITY

The most significant aspect of my encounter with my master was the realization that if Kabbalah's methods were achieved, we would experience the transformative event of immortality. We would learn that death was an illusion. Although death brought about a consciousness of deceased or departed people, in effect, these same people might well be alive. But, we ask ourselves, didn't we witness their death? No. We observed the interment.

Let me repeat that the previous observation of a deceased person comes about only by the use of our five senses. Science has already confirmed that dependency upon the five senses is unreliable. Most scientists take the unreliability of the five senses to its extreme and declare that the senses are not only unreliable, but actually interfere with our thought consciousness.

When we begin to recognize the limitations placed upon us by physical reality, we can embark upon a new adventure with our consciousness. Raising our awareness with the tools provided by Kabbalah, we can leave behind our body's limitations and soar to new dimensions never thought possible. As long as our old ways of thinking still enslave us to the limited programs thrust upon us by the Satan, we have no choice but to accept mortality. We are governed by the idea that seeing is believing, and seeing, as I have already demonstrated, is corrupt.

There will always remain die-hards who will not acquiesce to any radical, imaginative ideas. The Zohar states that when mortality ceases to be a reality, these die-hards will be subject to the rules of mortality. What is required is that a majority of the world's inhabitants remove the chaos that is mortality through a consciousness of immortality.

BRINGING IT ALL TOGETHER

Mortality, in essence, is an illusion.

What does this mean? Mortality, in essence, is an illusion. Nonetheless, until the majority comes to recognize it as such, we, who are left behind by a deceased person, will still feel the grief that accompanies death. When the death syndrome is exposed as a hoax and fraud perpetrated by the Satan to make us believe that death is irrevocable, then immortality will emerge and will become a reality that all shall notice.

Well, you might think, this doesn't sound like too difficult a task to handle. Who among us doesn't want to see our loved ones living eternally? The problem lies in the fact that the Satan is such a formidable enemy. He knows every trick in the chaos business. We can never underestimate his resourcefulness and clever intelligence. He's been at it since the time of Adam— and that's a long time.

When the Israelites forgot the message they had received, the Light force itself was dimmed. Physical reality again raised its terrible head and proclaimed its ascension to the throne. Consciousness of the soul would now take a back seat. Mortality joyously resumed its duties of putting the physical body to rest in the grave. The heavy stone that had been dominated by a Light force now assumed another dimension—the consciousness of the material.

The consciousness of the physical, material world as we now perceive it is of a temporary nature. Consequently, the death of a person comes about only as a result of the dominion of the physical body consciousness. Inasmuch as it is a temporary consciousness, it expresses the idea of mortality, that familiar environment in which everything—clothing, furniture, roads, bridges, all of physical reality—is subject to an end.

To assume that our clothing will never wear out, roads and bridges will never deteriorate—this is just a dream to some. As long as this concept remains nothing more than a dream, we are predetermining its continuation, seemingly without end. But the time for immortality is now.

THE BANISHMENT OF CHAOS AND THE RESTORATION OF ORDER

How can the battle of Light and darkness cease?

Although my doubtful nature at first made me hesitant to accept my master's revelations, we had enjoyed far too many experiences together during our seven-year relationship for me to remain wary. "Why not?" I asked, upon his introducing me to the immortality concept. During the early 20th century, American life expectancy was 48 years. Near the century's end, it was 81. Based on current experiments, some scientists have theorized that humankind's life span could be extended by decades, if not centuries. How? By altering genes. Of course, this notion of a dramatic extension of human life arouses healthy skepticism. We have heard such predictions before, and despite years of confident forecasts, there is still no cure for cancer. How, then, can the battle of Light and darkness cease? How will the peace of Kabbalah be attained? We must further examine the nature of mortality and the Satan's reign on Earth before we can speak of arriving at the ultimate moment—the moment of immortality.

SECTION III

THE ILLUSION
OF MORTALITY

THE MOST FRIGHTENING WORD

No word in any language brings greater fear into the heart than death. When this fear is compounded by the prospect of pain, suffering, or violence, panic ensues. Children are traumatized when their parents suddenly die in an automobile accident. A hiker holding the hand of his brother experiences the most terrible loss as he sees that hand slip away and his brother fall down the steep mountainside. Who can measure the grief so many people experience as they reach old age and approach the inevitable finale of death? This book aims to change our sense of mortality, to allow us to realize that we need to use our life span as an opportunity to connect with the Life force, the source of eternal vitality.

MAXWELL'S SECOND LAW OF THERMODYNAMICS

"Just because no one has heard your truth before, do not falter."
—*Rabbi Yehuda Brandwein*

At this time it may be wise to address questions undoubtedly in the reader's mind. These questions are understandable. Remember, I myself was tremendously shocked when, after all my years of rabbinical study, my master revealed to me the true purpose of what happened on Mount Sinai. Can you imagine how I felt when he told me that the true purpose of the revelation could be summed up in one word—immortality?

How could I have possibly been so receptive to this notion of immortality, of an end to death and suffering, when the master explained it to me? The reader may well wonder how I could even consider such a possibility in the face of my own life experiences. Have I never attended a funeral? Have I never been to a cemetery? I have lost dear members of my immediate family. I am familiar with mortality and the pain and suffering that follow the death of someone beloved.

When the moment of truth presented itself, I asked myself, "Why am I taking up such an enormous challenge?" On reflection I realized the magnitude of what I was trying to do: to allow the widespread study of Kabbalah to transform our environment to the point that death would no longer appear inevitable. I was well aware of the reaction my efforts in this area would be sure to provoke.

The teachings of Kabbalah have always appealed to the rational mind. Kabbalistic philosophies have stimulated individuals to change, but when you begin to tamper with the bedrock of reality, that is another matter. You are now shaking things up on a massive scale. You are bringing about a worldwide quake.

Therefore, I had to begin by asking myself: What exactly do I mean by bedrock of reality? What is the law of mortality and to what extent has it been proven?

Let us begin at the beginning. The basic law of physical reality is that of entropy—the idea that all things eventually fall apart, go downhill, die. This is Maxwell's Second Law of Thermodynamics, which states that everything of a physical, material nature must terminate in decay and death.

Now this Second Law of Thermodynamics has encountered no disagreement, debate, or rebuttal within the scientific community, but neither has this law ever been substantiated by critical scientific examination. The only evidence for the truth of Maxwell's Second Law of Thermodynamics is circumstantial. Despite scientists' usually sophisticated and technological methods, in this case their entire acceptance of this law rests upon the visual evidence of cars that finally have just too many miles on them, a favorite shirt that has been washed too many times and is finally not worth repairing, the degeneration of countless household items, and, most importantly, the green lawns of cemeteries stretching out to the horizon. The majority of the population has never questioned the acceptance of Maxwell's Second Law, for have we not also witnessed all these things? The painful funerals of our relatives and friends cannot be forgotten.

Yet, let me state here and now, as plainly as possible, that a conclusion that death is inevitable, based solely upon circumstantial evidence, is in direct opposition to the teachings of Kabbalah. Remember that it was the Satan who stated, "Repeat the lie one thousand times, and the world shall accept it as truth." The lie of mortality, the lie of death, has been repeated until we are literally blue in the face. I cannot repeat it now. Instead, I am going to repeat what my master told me when I wondered how I could ever attempt to share my understanding of immortality with my contemporaries: "When you believe that something is true and can benefit humankind, you must have the courage to withstand the onslaught of negative, unfounded criticism. Just because no one has heard your truth before, or the information has never before come into the public arena, do not falter."

These words continue to give me courage and appear to shine over this page as I write.

MASTER DECIPHERS THE COSMIC CODE FOR ME

Suddenly the words were on my tongue.

Of course, dear reader, I have some advantage over you, for the evidence you have experienced through your senses, may be only the evidence of cemeteries, of the disappearance of loved ones. For me, on the contrary, the vibrant memory of that day in the park in 1971 is more vivid than ever. My loved one—my master—did not disappear, but appeared, to me. My master was very real. He has been with me as a steady presence, varying only in intensity, since that first appearance. All of my experience since that time substantiates everything my master told me. His influence and steady guiding hand have been all I have needed to continue to have faith in my capacity to carry out the mission he entrusted to me.

Recall that he told me to prepare lectures for laypeople all over the world. Shortly after that time, I suddenly found myself delivering lectures at five in the morning without even having prepared for them. Today, it is 1,000 recorded tapes later. There have been many mornings when I faced my lecturing obligation with extreme fatigue. On those occasions I could hardly keep my eyes open or my head up. Yet suddenly the words were on my tongue; the information was flowing as continuously and clearly as if I had spent the entire previous day in preparation.

One of our centres, in Mexico City, arranged for me to give a nine-hour seminar there on a Sunday. When it came time to deliver my speech, I searched my briefcase only to discover that I had left my notes in New York. To add to the anxiety level, it turned out that Grupo Televison, Mexico's leading television station, would have a crew of five cameramen to record the entire seminar. When I turned to meditation and communion with my master, I asked him to provide me with nine hours of lecture material. He did not fail me.

I was to address an audience of 600 people. My English would be simultaneously translated into Spanish. My master, of course, spoke Yiddish rather than English. Thus any words he dictated to me would have to undergo immediate translation into two languages before reaching their target audience.

Did I display any nervousness as I took the podium? Yes, but my master calmed me, and true to his word, he plugged me right into the predestined and predetermined script that I delivered.

THE NATURE
OF KABBALISTIC TIME

Yesterday, today, and tomorrow are all in the here and now.

You see, the physicists were right. Yesterday, today, and tomorrow are all in the here and now. Rabbi Ashlag so beautifully stated, "Everything in this universe is like a seed of a tree. Everything of the future, the root, trunk, branches, leaves, even the fruit are included already within the seed, only awaiting their unfolding." This was precisely what I was doing at the seminar, unfolding that which was already prepared in a non-material realm. The seed contains the root on a non-material level. When the seed is planted, the root then reveals itself as a material, physical entity. The same may be said of the music on a recorded cassette or CD, which is in a non-material version until it is played and revealed as beautiful music to the ears of the listeners. In exactly this manner, I have been permitted to reveal knowledge that was destined to be revealed. I have been the boom box into which my master has inserted the particular tape or CD necessary for me to disseminate information on that special topic. The messages that my master gave me were sometimes so thrilling that I could not contain myself. I would marvel at entirely new pearls of wisdom he would pass along to me, and I would wonder at their origin.

Many times I could not remember what I had said only moments before. I had to be reminded of the words that had crossed my own lips. Then I needed to explain the words to inquiring students. This process kept my ego in its proper place. After all, it wasn't my material. It was handed to me.

I recall having read that Einstein did not receive the Nobel Prize for proving the general theory of relativity, but rather for having the imagination to consider such a theory. This is how I treat the information revealed through me. I am nothing more than the channel for this information, the means through which it is made available to the world. If I weren't that channel, someone else would be. To the amazement of my students, many of the secrets I have shared have shown up weeks after my lectures in the science section of the New York Times.

MIND OVER MATTER

When we change our former concept of 'death' as something absolute and irreversible, everything begins to make sense.

To understand how to free ourselves from the influence of mortality consciousness, my master told me, one must first become acquainted with the idea of mind over matter, a concept of critical importance here. Roughly 2,300 years after immortality's first chance in the Garden of Eden was lost when Adam ate from the Tree of Knowledge, immortality again had a brief moment on Mount Sinai, 3,400 years ago. Why did it take so long? What really happened when Adam ate that fruit?

We come here to the crux of the matter: we need to change our former concept of "death"—so absolute, so irreversible—to a concept of "the influence of mortality consciousness." When we do this, everything begins to make sense.

When Adam ate from the Tree of Knowledge, he did not lose his immortal nature altogether, but instead, he came under the influence of mortality consciousness. Life, as Adam knew it, would now be subject to ultimate death. There was no way for Adam and his offspring to achieve a sense of connection with eternity—immortality consciousness—even though he lived to be 930 years old! The Satan's hand had too deeply touched Adam's consciousness for him to change it through self-discipline. Adam's DNA had been altered to include the gene of mortality, which would be transferred to his offspring. However, just as the potential for avoiding certain genetic diseases has been tapped by scientists as they continue to map DNA, so the potential for immortality is still within human DNA. It is only in our own time that scientists have been exploring genetic engineering. Soon the genetic code of immortality will be deciphered, and the potential for reversing the aging process may be realized. When will this happen?

NO PAIN, NO GAIN

Every cloud has a silver lining.

The Zohar states that a spiritual cleansing was experienced by humanity with the Mount Sinai event. At that time, close to 3,400 years ago, the consciousness of the people reversed itself to the Tree of Life-reality of immortality. The clues to accessing this reversal are encoded in the Bible. Unfortunately, states the Zohar, the narratives included in the Bible—such as the history of Noah's ark and the flood, the Tower of Babel, and the Israelites' bondage in Egypt—are treated as nothing more than fables. In essence, these were the three incidents of tragedy that culminated in the reversal of death consciousness. In each of these experiences, the participants were humbled by the realization that we were not in control. Just as later, in 1490 and 1940, the wholesale displacement of populations would break open the illusionary security of daily life to provide an opportunity of realizing our true nature, so, too, these trials of Biblical times laid the foundation for a redemption from the fearful behavior of the Israelites, who had been too impatient to wait for Moses and had created the Golden Calf to take his place. Every cloud has a silver lining. All of these challenging experiences brought with them an opportunity for the transition from mortality consciousness to one of immortality consciousness.

After surviving something as devastating as the flood that carried Noah's ark, the people were prepared for Mount Sinai. Their egos went by the wayside. It was only Pharaoh who was still dominated by his ego to the extent that he expressed a skeptical, "show-me" attitude when it came to the claims of Moses. All he cared about was the surface magic, and both the Egyptian magicians and Moses could transform the things he was capable of seeing. The consciousness of the Israelites went much deeper; it had been unlocked to receive the Light force. This was an evolutionary process that had to be in place before the Light force could begin to be accessed.

THE REMOVAL OF THE MORTALITY INFLUENCE

The mortality influence at the time of the Garden of Eden penetrated to the genetic level.

The mortality influence goes deep; as I have indicated above, mortality at the time of the Garden of Eden penetrated to the genetic level. Two distinct stages are required for its removal. The first is for us to become prepared for the transformation, to cease doubting. We must leave our cynicism and "show-me" egos behind, and change over to certainty consciousness. And after this we must allow ourselves to receive the radical metaphysical alteration that we undergo when we truly open ourselves to Kabbalah energy. We must, of our own free will, choose immortality.

THE CHOICE OF IMMORTALITY

God and the Light force exist in perpetuity.

When Adam opted for the Tree of Knowledge and became infused with mortality consciousness, our connection with eternity was weakened. Yet God and the Light force exist in perpetuity. Since we are part of God, eternity is an inherent part of us. When Adam fell under the influence of mortality through employing his free will to choose the Tree of Knowledge over the Tree of Life, the gene for immortality was more or less informed that its services were no longer required. While initially this may seem like a shocking statement, "mind over matter" is very much being verified by science today. Scientists have documented that practitioners of yoga can raise body temperature many degrees above normal. Meditation and positive thinking have been scientifically proven in double-blind studies to strengthen the immune system. So, this is another case of science catching up with Kabbalah.

NO COERCION IN SPIRITUALITY

*Why, when our gut feeling tells us not to do something,
do we sometimes disregard this internal advice
and go ahead and do it anyway?*

Within human nature, free will is essential. The doctrine of "no coercion in spirituality" that was established at the time of original Creation, governed and guided God and the Godlike feature within us all. If Adam was foolish enough not to pay attention to the warning of his internal, Godlike component, then his desire for mortality superseded the integral aspect of immortality.

Why, when our gut feeling tells us not to do something, do we sometimes disregard this internal advice and go ahead and do it anyway? Free will is part of us. The only problem with free will is that we also have as our sidekick, the Satan's chaotic consciousness, which became an equal partner in our decision-making process. Naturally, the Satan pushes his consciousness of mortality—and he has the cemeteries as proof of his success!

We do have free will to choose immortality, however. Until the idea of Mount Sinai immortality penetrated my consciousness, I, too, fell under the mortality consciousness of the Satan. However, with the passing of time, as my master had predicted,

I began to take this matter very seriously. I would now be prepared to share this wonderful opportunity of immortality with the world. This reality could not come to pass until I reached a level of certainty consciousness.

If our minds actually control our very existence, even to the extent of immortality, how is the consciousness of humanity going to change? It hasn't for over 5,700 years, except for a short interval of 40 days between the time of revelation and the Golden Calf incident!

THE MEANING OF THE GOLDEN CALF

*Some of the answers will require
more data from science.*

Some important questions need to be answered: What actually happened when the Israelites created the Golden Calf and were thereby thrust back into the abyss of mortality that is still with us today? Why and how did these Israelites sink into the depths of deception in assuming that the Golden Calf would replace Moses, the miracle man? How could that second opportunity for choosing immortality pass out of people's hands, particularly given the great leadership of Moses?

These and other questions of this nature needed clarification before I could possibly understand the deeper meaning of immortality. When I asked them of my master, he responded to some of my inquiries and stated that others would require more data from science before they could become comprehensible to the layperson.

The Golden Calf was deeply frightening at the time it was created, my master explained. For the Golden Calf, in fact, appeared to come to life, and God instructed Moses to slay the Israelites who responded to the living Golden Calf as some kind of god. He also instructed Moses to obliterate the molten Golden Calf.

Yet the Golden Calf that appeared to come to life would not have the same terrifying effect today. Such fear of mechanical beings that "come to life" is also inherent in the story of the Golem, made out of earth by Rabbi Loew of Prague, a Kabbalist. This Golem was created to serve man, went out of control, and began to act from its own agency, but the story was hardly taken seriously.

The film industry is another instance of our visual senses appearing to witness the creation of life, for with the creation of cinema, the actors were suddenly present in the movie palace, although they were not there. A machine producing light and sound animated these performers.

We do not assume that because these machines appear so animated that they are gods. How then could the Israelites have been so duped?

The Zohar also states that when the tablets crashed to the ground and shattered, the short-lived reality of immortality came to an abrupt end. How was this possible?

Unfortunately, after the revelation on Mount Sinai, the power of certainty was not firmly entrenched in the consciousness of the Israelites. When Moses did not return when they had expected, they went ahead and explored a replacement for Moses. Did they not trust that Moses would keep his word? Why were they so willing to discard the miracles that Moses had been instrumental in achieving for their benefit? The Israelites were truly an enlightened people and knew all about the power of the mind. So what happened?

THE SATAN'S INFLUENCE

It is Kabbalah that is miraculous.

Although the Biblical account makes no mention of them, among those who left Egypt with the Israelites were some people it would have been better to leave behind. The Kabbalah refers to them as the Erev Rav—hateful people trained in the practice of Egyptian magic and consumed with a desire to receive for the self alone. Despite their corrupt nature, they were highly skilled.

Two of the darkest of these magicians were Yunus and Yumbrus. They had learned their trade from the master magician, the Satan, and had waited a long time for this opportunity. When Moses did not return, they could seize power.

They practiced a real magic. It was not the kind demonstrated by stage illusionists who appear to pull a bird out of a hat or have their body sawed in half.

With Moses gone, the Erev Rav were the ones who whipped up the Israelites, arousing their clamor for a man-god. After 40 days of grumbling and dissatisfaction that Moses had abandoned them in the desert, the people were vulnerable to negativity. Moses was a miracle by, and within, himself. The Golden Calf, which could breathe and move and speak, was a mechanistic marvel, and the Israelites found it easy to forget the true miracle.

The problem with the Israelites was one related to the history of their free will. Their consciousness had been locked into slavery for generations, and they were therefore always in need of someone or something that could relieve them of any and all responsibilities. They were incapable of assuming total accountability. Their consciousness was such that they were not prepared to be blamed for any decisions they might make, for fear of becoming a failure. This was their attitude toward Moses. He would have always been there when they were looking for a scapegoat. So when the idea of a Golden Calf was presented by Yunus and Yumbrus, the Israelites seized this opportunity out of weakness.

The creation of an animated, vocal Golden Calf was regarded as a stunning miracle 3,400 years ago. Today, however, this would surprise no one. Yunus and Yumbrus were simply more than three millennia ahead of their time. What the Israelites referred to in their day as magic is now called technology. We have robotic welders on the automotive assembly line, talking computers, and even alarm systems for our automobiles that will, at the approach of an intruder, shout warnings at us.

Experience with Kabbalah will allow us to realize that it is the Light force that is miraculous. As the level of consciousness rises, achievements, such as the cloning of parts of our bodies to repair weakened or damaged hearts and organs, will seem to be the natural application of technology by enlightened beings capable of exerting a highly refined level of control over their own lives through consciousness. The choice for immortality will be seen in the same light.

THE TREE OF KNOWLEDGE OR THE TREE OF LIFE?

The moment for choosing immortality appears to have arrived.

Despite people's desire for immortality, until now, the rule of mind over matter has not been sufficient to remove the influence of mortality consciousness. After meditating on this matter for some time, I asked my master why this was so.

The response was slow in coming. My master looked into my eyes with penetrating energy. I was certain he felt the difficulty that I would have in understanding the concept he was about to reveal, and I felt that he was using the quiet power of his wisdom to eliminate the metaphysical obstacles hindering my comprehension.

"Our rational minds, unfortunately, have very little sway or influence over our activities, our bodies, or our environment. In fact, our rational minds, more times than not, produce the chaos and uncertainty in our lives. Where we do exercise some measure of control is in determining whether we choose the Tree of Life or the Tree of Knowledge. Translated into simple terms, our consciousness has two directions of thought that can be taken. We can make an attempt to exercise a desire to receive for the sake of sharing that which we receive, or we can have a desire to receive for the self alone."

There is no question that for every activity expressed and manifested on the physical level of activity, there has been a prior thought or intention behind it. Our hands do not move without being commanded to do so by our minds. A hand will not raise or lower itself by its own choice. Even the process of breathing is determined by our minds.

There is an inherent intelligence to the Light force. In the final analysis, it is the Light force within us that heals a broken bone; it is not the orthopedist. We have free will to direct the Light force. Immortality energy has always been present, and certainty consciousness is all that is necessary to make that potential energy an actual energy. However, because of the doctrine "no coercion in spirituality," free choice must be exercised. The moment of such a choice appears to have arrived.

NEAR-DEATH EXPERIENCES

What exactly is death?

Many vivid near-death experiences (NDEs) have been recorded in medical literature around the world. With advanced medical technology, more and more patients are journeying back from the edge of death. These experiences have brought the discussion of mortality into the general public discourse. What exactly is death? How can we know that a person has actually died?

We have heard of those rare occasions where people in catatonic states have been buried, or when morticians have observed a supposedly dead body in a sweat. It is known that the hair and nails of someone declared legally dead continue to grow. Some patients in a comatose state and on life-supporting instruments appear to be functioning in the unconscious realm after the plug has been pulled. This has been measured through monitoring their brain-waves.

The Zohar is replete with near-death experiences. It even states the procedure for those found on the line between life and death. Almost all people who have suffered clinical death and then recovered report journeying through a long tunnel with Light at the end of it. We are told in the Zohar that upon the death of the physical body, the soul immediately travels to Hebron, where Adam died approximately 4,800 years ago. The soul makes this journey by means of a long tunnel.

Those whose time has not come, however, are sent back to regain their consciousness and resume life among the living. What these people also report is a life-review experience and the presence of deceased relatives. Each of these experiences is discussed in the Zohar.

After these patients have regained consciousness, they tell of the attending physicians' efforts to save them. They recount exactly the position of each person in the room, what each was doing and saying. They describe themselves as hovering over the bed where they see themselves lying. They recount the procedure associated with the revival of their physical bodies. These observations have often been made while they were legally dead.

The Satan, ever the trickster, clothes death in robes of terror. He paints a picture of the skeletal grim reaper with a scythe in his bony hand. He whispers that death is a dark and inescapable finality—a lonely corridor down which all must walk and none return.

As ever, the Satan is a liar.

The many recorded NDEs provide a picture that is in direct conflict with what the majority of people believe about death. This is precisely why the Satan is the master trickster. For millennia, he has fooled Earth's inhabitants into believing that death is the only reality that never changes. The master magician has convinced us that chaos is an unchangeable reality and that death is an indisputable truth.

Why haven't the researchers of NDEs made their findings known among laypeople? It is because the Satan has employed the finest and most well-intentioned scientists to do his bidding. Even when the evidence contradicts the common notion of what death really is and means, the Satan persists.

SIR JAMES JEANS: NO REALITY BUT THOUGHT

Kabbalah includes information on how to bridge the two worlds of consciousness and physical reality.

When the consciousness of the Israelites took a turn toward uncertainty, the Golden Calf was the result. The power of consciousness, my master said, is the most potent weapon at the disposal of humankind. As Sir James Jeans, the Nobel laureate physicist, has stated, in our reality: In our universe, there is nothing more than consciousness. He has written that the universe is beginning to look more like a big thought than a big machine. The physical universe can, in fact, interfere with reality.

Surprisingly, my master knew what the scientist is only now beginning to know and understand. The physicist continues to face a gap between the theory and its application. The Kabbalist has no problem. Kabbalah includes information on how to bridge the two worlds of consciousness and physical reality.

THE MISTAKE OF MOUNT SINAI

A dogmatic form of religion was never the intention of revelation.

When my master discussed the revelation on Mount Sinai, he said that soon the circumstances would appear in which I would receive my confirmation that immortality was real. I felt that he was referring to what Karen and I established as the Mount Sinai revelation experience. By the late 1970s, these gatherings included scholars who were Kabbalah-educated and initiated, although the conferences were open to all who could raise their consciousness to the level of acceptance of immortality.

Many of the established Jewish communities were opposed to linking this event to Shavuot. They asked that we redesignate the event as the "giving of the Ten

Commandments" and that we omit the word "immortality." When I indicated that this event was less my own idea, but instead embodied conclusions reached by the Zohar, the hostility became still more intense. However, I knew that there was no turning back, for the traditional methods of observation of this holiday ignored the Zohar. My master believed, and I believe, that a dogmatic form of religion was never the intent of the revelation. Neither was the revelation intended as an event in which the Jewish people became a nation shaped from a previous horde of slaves.

The purpose of the revelation was instead to restore the universe to an orderly, structured nature—a world where the Life force is law, as it existed before Adam. To any rational mind, this new approach was exactly what people wanted and needed. Why would this interpretation of the revelation bring down the terrible wrath of the Jewish establishment and a hostility between Jews only seen during the destruction of the Temples? This is even more incomprehensible to me when I consider that immortality is a concept accepted within all major religions.

THE PROACTIVITY OF CERTAINTY CONSCIOUSNESS

*To be truly proactive requires being aware
of what is happening at all times.*

Doubt and negative thinking perpetuate our lack of connection with the Light force. Doubt—individual, collective, or global—might as well be the name of the Satan, the master magician. He can convince us of impending disaster when disaster is only in our heads. He creates the illusion of imminent chaos to instill in our minds doubt about the future. This illusion prevents us from seizing the chance to overcome chaos in our lives.

Our consciousness level has been reduced by the Satan so that we come to believe that circumstances, other people, and our bodies, are responsible for all the chaos we experience. For this reason, we are unprepared for the approach of disaster. We relinquish control. We become reactive individuals. When circumstances improve, our egos are reassured. It appears that we have become proactive, but our renewed confidence is merely the result of circumstances outside ourselves. We are stimulated by the unexpected success. This illusion that we have become proactive is another demonstration of how cunning the Satan is. He has taken a reactive situation and convinced us that we are proactive, that we have regained mastery over our destiny.

To be truly proactive, in constant control over our destinies, requires an elevated consciousness of what is really going on at all times. Our goal is to achieve this proactive nature. When everything around us is crumbling, however, the Satan gets high marks for his performance of illusion. He has convinced us that we are controlled by the chaotic condition.

THE ZOHAR'S INTERPRETATION OF THE BIBLE

All we need to eliminate chaos from our lives is a change in consciousness.

When I began to understand that mastery of Kabbalah was the means of greater connection with the Light force, I began to notice many difficult sections in the Zohar pointing out that mortality does not apply to everyone. Sections of the Zohar that I had studied for years suddenly had new and profound levels of meaning.

The first passage of the Zohar that I came across that was of this nature concerned Jacob, the third and greatest of the Biblical patriarchs. Jacob had a very long life, and he left the physical environment we call reality only when he chose to do so. Although the Bible appears to indicate that Jacob did die, I became certain that the passages actually meant that he no longer was in contact with our familiar physical reality. He was embalmed and in contact with a greater reality.

In fact, the placing of Jacob in the cave in the field of Machpelah, near Mamre, which Avraham had bought as a burial site, was done to create the illusion of death, just as a magician covers a bird cage and then causes the bird to vanish. Clearly the implication of such a magic trick is that the bird has left to appear in another location.

For Jacob, it was those left behind who vanished. The sight of people wailing over his grave must have been strange to Jacob, who clearly had achieved the state that Kabbalists refer to as living in the Tree of Life reality.

Death, a revealment showing us there that there is no death, thus becomes the greatest illusion of all. We, the audience, are those who are left behind.

My master's sudden reappearance in the park two years after his supposed departure from this life was only one proof of this truth. His continual appearances since that time have provided me with miraculous and incredible support. Death, for my master, as with Jacob the patriarch, revealed for us that there is no death. Death is merely a door through which Jacob and my master had passed to reach the realm of truth. To understand this viewpoint will require a complete overhaul of our previous perspective concerning chaos and death. All we need to eliminate chaos from our lives is a change in consciousness.

HEALING THROUGH THE LIGHT FORCE

*The patient must rid his or her body
of the negative entities.*

Only after I fully understood this paradoxical condition did I relate it to the cancers that afflict humankind. The culprit in illness is the Satan. In his quest for sustenance, he begins to drain off the Light force from the sick person. The Light force continues to retreat as the disease progresses. The affliction is a result of the Satan's presence, with his negative entities. The patient must rid his or her body of the negative entities.

How do we combat a metaphysical enemy that we cannot see or observe? This is exactly what Kabbalah is all about. Its secret codes unlock the metaphysical barriers to an all-out war with these enemies of humanity. I am not implying that the medical profession has no place in our society, but doctors do not address the origin and causes of our maladies. With the dawning of the 21st century, however, Kabbalah will make its grand entrance onto the stage of human history.

THE SEARCH TODAY FOR CONTINUAL VITALITY

A birthday is an opportunity to connect with the secret of life.

Medical science is aware of the constant recreation of every facet of our physical body. We are not the same person physically seven years after birth. As we move into our 20s and 30s, this regeneration slows down and our bodies begin to deteriorate. Kabbalistically, we understand why the regenerating process should be in seven-year cycles. If the process of regeneration could be continual, there would be no reason we could not live forever.

How are we to remove these illusions of aging and death from our consciousness? We must elevate our consciousness and achieve a heightened awareness. We must question and, above all, accumulate knowledge and information.

The regenerating process that is so evident with birth is impressive in displaying our natural capacity for self-rejuvenation. The fact that we have not yet understood how that original system works so well should not force us into thinking that we cannot learn.

The Kabbalah Centre celebrates this connection with our original capacity for self-regeneration through making birthdays an occasion for community celebration and connection. Usually, a birthday party is a reminder that we are "getting older." Another year has passed. To draw darkness over our fear of old age, by custom, we blow out the lights of the candles.

A birthday at the Kabbalah Centre is an opportunity to go back to the future. We connect to that moment when we took our first breath of air. Time is heading forward to the moment when it all began. This is a Kabbalistic, cyclic interpretation of time. It is always circular. A fruit seed moves forward in time and motion only to become the seed of the fruit from which it grew. When one applies one's rational mind to trying to comprehend such a cycle, one runs into trouble. "After the fruit tree has given birth to the fruit," I asked my master, "why must there be a whole new process of budding, producing the flower again, and then finally the fruit?"

"The answer," responded my master, "is the secret of life itself."

A birthday is an opportunity to connect with that secret. The anniversary day reminds us that our origin of strength and future development has returned to us. We can cast aside our preoccupation with day-to-day trivialities and remember how wonderful it is simply to be alive. The Light force returns in full again, as it appeared during our first moment of life. As we are forced into greater preoccupation in relation to the material world, we accommodate the Satan more as we get older. As part of our birthday ceremonies, we go back to that moment of birth and shed the physical realities of the Satan.

Our consciousness has control over matter. On our birthdays we can shed the trappings of 365 physical days—days in which we have added negativity and caused the Light force's withdrawal. We can connect with and celebrate the energy of our beginnings.

MORTALITY IS HELPLESS BEFORE CONSCIOUSNESS

There is nothing out there but consciousness.

In this, the dawn of the new millennium, we will come to a collective realization that there is nothing out there but consciousness. At this level of understanding, chaos, ill health, financial failure, and all the rest of the dismal consequences of Murphy's Law will be seen for what they are—illusionary manifestations of mind and consciousness. In short, they are figments of our imagination, and when that is realized on a broad scale, the Angel of Death, the Satan, finally will be conquered.

REMOVING THE LAYERS
OF ILLUSION

To understand the nature of the physical world requires that we make connections with the metaphysical realm of existence. The metaphysical is not really a world beyond. It is right here, now, and the purpose of Kabbalah is to peel away the layers of illusion so that we may connect with the internal realm of the Light force.

We base our sense of reality upon our immediate perceptions; yet our perceptions are often perceptions of an illusory world of appearances.

The Zohar compares the death of the patriarch Jacob to the sun's path at nightfall. This is a beautiful analogy. Our sensory perception of the setting of the sun is in fact a consequence of the rotation of the earth. When we watch the romantic setting of the sun, are we therefore to understand that what we are seeing is not real?

No, the material world of appearances has its own reality. What the Zohar provides us with is the connection to truth so that we shall not be entirely captured by this material and illusionary world of appearances. This means that if we become caught up in the dominance of the physical, material world, we have surrendered to the consciousness of chaos and the

Satan and forsaken our chance to defeat the idea of mortality and chaos. It is that simple and clear. If what I have just said seems unclear, permit me to repeat the theme that weaves through this entire book.

The laws of the physical realm are not the cause of the things we observe. There is no disagreement about what has been seen. Science says that what you see is reality—but not because your eyes see it. The eyes are not the cause of what you see. The eyes, being physical, cannot determine what we see. What we believe, or what is in our consciousness, determines what we see. Two people observing the same accident can disagree about who is to blame, although the two observers are equally near the accident. Why is this? Perhaps one observer prefers Fords to Chevrolets and becomes angered at seeing the Ford totaled. He blames the driver of the Chevrolet. The other observer likes Chevrolets and so decides that the Ford driver had been careless.

What is in the consciousness determines the outcome. The cause begins within consciousness, an immaterial realm. For Kabbalist and the student trained in the study of Kabbalah, the sun did not disappear in the evening. Its disappearance was not related to its physical appearance. The sun, states the Zohar, at an appointed time (sunset) discontinues its intrinsic characteristic of sharing beneficence. The night is nothing more than the sun's desire (consciousness) to discontinue shedding its light on earth, and now the moon has the opportunity to act as a conduit of light.

Conventional interpretation and the Zohar do not disagree as to whether the sun is shining. It does not shine at nightfall. What the Zohar is trying to impress upon us is the importance of searching out the real reason, which will always lie in the immaterial, non-physical realm of reality. For too long, humanity has looked to the physical world for data. What the Zohar is stating is that we shall never find complete answers on this physical level. We must reach out to the immaterial realm of the spirit, where reality is never illusion.

We have become so far removed from the realm of pure thought, instead relying on visual evidence, that we have lost access to that realm. We no longer depend on the power of the mind and consciousness. It is no wonder that the Satan prefers we remain unconscious and continue these millennia of chaos, earthquakes, volcanoes, tornadoes, and floods. These disasters appear to be proof positive that the physical realm controls us and we are helpless in the face of it.

The Zohar, however, does not believe that we are helpless. We can control all of these so-called natural disasters. First, we must know why they occur.

At first, this may seem absurd. How do you know you cannot control disasters? Have you ever tried it? Are you afraid of what people might think of you? Or do you think your loved ones will begin to investigate ways of having you committed?

Another question: Why and how did you come to the conclusion that the source of natural disasters is God—an immaterial, nonphysical entity? When was the last time you saw God? On what physical data is such a conclusion based?

The Satan has done a brilliant job with all. We think about God only when things are bad, so as to keep us away from the truth about mind over matter—including our powers over earthquakes, volcanoes, and floods. The Satan might even be in deep trouble if we didn't blame God.

When we have brought our consciousness to its rightful place, we shall have traveled 99 percent of the road to the elimination of chaos and mortality. Once we have achieved this level of consciousness, then we will approach the remaining one percent—the knowledge of how to once and for all remove the Satan from our lives. This revelation is forthcoming.

SECTION IV

IMMORTALITY NOW

RECOGNIZING A NEW DIMENSION

At 3:00 a.m. during the winter of 1995, in our home in New York, the phone rang. It was a frantic student telephoning me from Los Angeles. My sons, Yehuda and Michael, and I were at our usual study session and discussing our scheduled flight to Los Angeles at 4:00 p.m. that afternoon. Although it is not unusual for students and friends from around the world to call at such an hour, I sensed that this call was different.

The student told me that her family had just received word from the hospital that a cousin of hers had just died. He had been partying at a home in Malibu when he had stepped out to the veranda, situated high above the Pacific, with other friends. The pillar supports of the veranda had collapsed under the weight of the people, and the student's cousin and the others had gone tumbling down into the water. The student's cousin was killed.

"Why are you calling?" I asked. I thought she might request that I deliver a eulogy.

"I am calling you so that you will bring my cousin back to life," she said.

I was dumbstruck. "What made you think that I

can resurrect the dead?" I asked. "I've never even made an attempt at restoring life to someone who has died. I wouldn't know how to begin such an action." Furthermore, although it is recorded in the Zohar that Rabbi Shimon bar Yochai and others were capable of accomplishing such an extraordinary feat, I didn't have the slightest idea of how to begin.

She tearfully pleaded with me to attend the funeral the next afternoon at 2:00 p.m. I asked for the dead man's name and the names of his parents, and with that the conversation ended.

I asked the boys what they thought of the conversation. The three of us turned toward the picture of my master. We were confident that my master would provide us with what the entire episode meant and especially what were we to do.

Without any prior knowledge, my master asked, "Are you aware of whose death anniversary is this evening? It is the death anniversary of Rabbi Avraham Azulai, the 16th-century Kabbalist."

My master referred me to the writings of Rabbi Avraham Azulai concerning the year 2000, which corresponds to the biblical calendar year of 5760. Although the year 5760 doesn't have any deep significance—certainly nothing close to the excitement expressed about the 2,000-year millennium—

nonetheless, what Rabbi Azulai revealed concerning resurrection by the year 2000 was mind-boggling.

I knew that my master was responding to our dilemma concerning the request to revive the student's young cousin and restore him back to life, and I realized that Rabbi Azulai would be with us if we requested his assistance.

My son, Yehuda, immediately searched and found the volume of Rabbi Azulai's work that dealt with the year 2000. When Yehuda opened the book, without looking for any particular subject, he couldn't believe what he was looking at. Michael and I both saw the expression on his face.

"You're not going to believe what I turned to," stammered Yehuda. He was shaking like a leaf.

Michael and I looked at each another and then at Yehuda.

"Immortality!"

In the next few moments, as my sons and I collected our wits, we realized a whole new dimension of the subject of immortality. We realized that the reality of eternal life was not awaiting God's decision as to when it was going to happen. It would depend upon humankind's consciousness and effort to create this reality.

This was a far cry from what I had been led to believe throughout my adult life. Prayers recited each day invoked the mercy of the Creator to please bring an end to death and chaos. Nothing had led me to understand that the realization of immortality grew out of man's desire and effort.

The first step was to accept the idea that immortality was a matter that people must deal with themselves. If their consciousness was asleep or ignorant, then immortality could be a long time in coming. Rabbi Azulai provided the first of many steps to draw the curtain down on the illusionary stage of mortality.

Suddenly the conversations I had had with the master some 30 years before meant something deeper to me. In one evening, someone requested that I restore life to a deceased person, and I suddenly became aware that immortality was an idea whose time had come.

Were we going to remain spectators at the crossroads of human history, or were we going to extend our hands and grasp the moment?

My sons and I were frightened by the prospect of driving a further wedge between ourselves and the establishment. What would be their response this time? Although the idea of immortality is not new to religionists, the thought that we, the people, are the instruments by which this concept will become a reality will probably be too difficult for them to accept.

The message was clear, however. Our mission was to create an atmosphere for immortality acceptance. We had to destroy one of the Satan's most formidable weapons against humanity—death. We knew, of course, that my master and Rabbi Azulai would be there for us when the need arose.

What is truly amazing is the enormous flow of data that continued to feed the effort to raise the world consciousness toward immortality. Piece by piece, the puzzle began to unfold, and before we knew it, the concept of immortality, normally a great taboo in the medical sciences, took on an air of respectability. Biotech research produced the immortality enzyme. The press began to discuss the possibility of never-ending life. Books, written by physicists espousing immortality and resurrection, suddenly appeared in the bookstores. The fever surrounding immortality reached new heights.

On that evening on which I received our calling, it struck us that the young man who had lost his life had the same name as Rabbi Azulai: Avraham. It was a telling coincidence. The father of the decreased was named was Yigal, which means, "and he shall free or cause to be liberated." This is precisely what Rabbi Azulai had in mind—that the world would be liberated from death and chaos.

WHAT GOD TOLD ADAM AND EVE

Living in a world where mortality appears inevitable, a person seeking the wisdom of the spiritual realm might study the Bible and conclude that God told Adam and Eve not to eat from the Tree of Knowledge or they would die.

A person turning to Kabbalah, however, is able to understand that the Bible, as my master explained, is "nothing more than a coded instrument to reach the essential understanding of how mortality came into existence." What was God trying to warn Adam and Eve about, if not death—a permanent, irreversible extinguishing of all life?

He was trying to warn them that they would connect, through that fruit, with the illusionary realm of limitation, fragmentation, and death consciousness. They would become vulnerable to that same glittering world of material goods and corruption in which we live today.

But what world are we living in? Kabbalah makes it clear that whether the Satan succeeded in his quest was left to Adam and Eve in accordance with the doctrine of free will. God knew that they would become subject to the illusionary realm of death consciousness, but he also knew that Adam and Eve's descendants would still continue to have a choice.

We are the descendants of Adam and Eve. We have a choice. If we study Kabbalah, we become aware that we have a choice. This book is written to ask you the question (remember Kabbalists are always asking questions), "Do you, dear reader, choose immortality?"

FAITH ALLOWS US TO NOT REPEAT OUR MISTAKES

Humankind will commence the restoration of a chaotic world.

The last moment of connection with the Tree of Life reality was lost when the Israelites, as they waited for Moses to come down from Mount Sinai, became impatient and were shaken in their faith. As I have explained, the fact that the revelation's purpose was to reveal our immortality was made clear to me by my master, who charged me with sharing this knowledge not only with those traditionally allowed to study Kabbalah, not only with the Orthodox, not only with Jews, but in fact, with all of humanity.

I will admit to being somewhat intimidated initially by the enormity of this task. But as I began to understand what opportunity was lost at Mount Sinai and what opportunity was gained, and to consider the fact that I had been born at this extraordinarily opportune historical moment, I began to go deeper and deeper into this mystery of eternal life. Just what did it mean? In this questioning, I naturally turned to my master.

In response, he opened the Zohar and turned to a passage that at first appeared obtuse. He explained that this section dealt with the night when the Decalogue was revealed. Rabbi Shimon, the author of the Zohar, was carrying on a discussion with his companions. He revealed with excitement, for the first time in history, that with proper meditations, the secret of one aspect of immortality would begin to become part of the landscape of human civilization. Humankind would commence the restoration of a chaotic world. The Satan would no longer feel the comfort of monopolizing and manipulating humankind. He would begin to be defensive. No longer would people have to pray to God that they be on His good side and therefore, be lucky to avoid the chaos all around them.

I waited patiently for my master's interpretation of this revelation. Did I understand correctly that death would be forced to take a holiday? "Yes," he replied. "Within this Zohar gleamed the secret of one aspect of immortality." He went on to tell me exactly how the switch of the Light force can be turned on.

Before I continue in that vein, let me review some basic Kabbalistic principles.

TOMORROW IS INCLUDED IN THE PAST

Everything is already present;
it must only be properly nurtured and allowed to unfold.

Yet again, let us take up the story of Adam and Eve and the fruit. I have stated that the crux of the matter lies in our changing our former concept of death—so absolute, so irreversible—to a concept of the influence of mortality consciousness. I stated that when we do this, everything begins to make sense.

This is because whether or not our minds grasp the full implications of immortality—the slowing down of time—the fact remains that immortality exists and has been confirmed. That was what the Revelation at Mt. Sinai was about! Immortality now awaits the acceptance of anyone willing to grasp the concept.

You may also remember that one does not arrive at embracing this concept through the rational mind. As I explained earlier, a seed moves forward in time and shape only to become the seed of the fruit from which it first grew. My master stated that the reason for such a cycle is, in fact, the secret of life itself.

Another way of describing this secret, cyclic nature of time is to say, "Tomorrow is included in the past." Everything is already present; it must only be properly nurtured and allowed to unfold.

Scientists have only recently come to understand that much of the future pattern of growth of an organism is already programmed within the genes of that organism. The master Kabbalists had discovered this secret well in advance of the scientists. After all, where did the tree come from if not from the seed? Most of us cannot "read" the seed and see that it will grow into the tree. So, too, at the present time, most of us cannot "read" our tomorrows. We are, therefore, subject to many uncertainties.

Yet the scientists, unfortunately, are confined to theory. Although they have arrived at a particular knowledge of the future by looking at a particular seed and examining its particular genetic makeup, they cannot transfer such an ability to their own lives in general or those of their neighbors. On a practical level, they are like the rest of us, for if they could see into the future in a more general sense, they would all become immensely wealthy. They would purchase stock today and know that prices would go up tomorrow. (The only people now able to do this with certainty are subject to arrest for insider trading!)

Scientists have built telescopes powerful enough to see stars that, in fact, disappeared long before our lifetime. They can see far, far into the past, but they must wait for Kabbalists to reveal the information of how to see equally well into the future.

"One day," my master said to me, "you shall share with the world the secrets of how to achieve immortality. All it takes is information and 'certainty consciousness' to bring this phenomenon to fruition."

Then and there, I made him a promise that I would never falter in my certainty consciousness, and I would not let him down.

THE OBSTACLE COURSE OF ENLIGHTENMENT

"The universe has a beat and a rhythm."
—*Rabbi Yehuda Brandwein*

I do not expect that people will accept the concept of immortality overnight. It takes time for major discoveries made by specialists—in this case, Kabbalists—to penetrate into the general population's consciousness. As I have said before, however, it is necessary to have patience. After all, when one has a different sense of time, how "long" are we really having to wait? Scientists themselves, who are behind Kabbalah here, have greatly expanded the human sense of time, and they themselves realize that even evolutionary time baffles the imagination. Some natural history museums have a particular way of trying to overcome the difficulty the rational mind has in comprehending even the time span involved from the date of the oldest fossils until our own era. They display the life of the universe in the image of a clock, with 12 as the beginning of recorded prehistory. On this clock, human life doesn't even start until the very last minute before 12!

In the realm of Kabbalah, however, we aren't talking about the last minute, but about one of the first in the comprehension of eternity. The heightened awareness of eternity within the mainstream of humanity must itself undergo a gradual, evolutionary process.

As the reader by now knows, spreading the word about contact with eternity was given to me as my mission, my task. "The universe has a beat and a rhythm," said my master. "You will have to pay careful attention to its sound, and only then will you become familiar with information that reaches us all the time, if we only listen."

This was a sweet tune to my ears, but I often realize that this statement of my master's, like so many others, had nuances of meaning that have only unfolded with time. What did my master have in mind about listening carefully to the musical strings of the universe? At the time, I was relatively new to Kabbalah, and never anticipated that there would be objections to a good thing.

Little did I realize the heartbreak that must accompany students of Kabbalah along their spiritual journeys. Many people rejected the idea of immortality out of hand, without even entertaining it as a possibility. I was to truly learn what it means to be patient.

Sometimes it seems to me that no other teachings of spirituality have had to endure the obstacles and roadblocks that have been placed in the way of the dissemination of the wisdom of Kabbalah. Undoubtedly, many people, even with good intentions, will assist the Satan in his effort to halt Kabbalah. (How ironic that a popular expression has the road to Hell being paved with good intentions!) However, the master often reminded me that certainty and truthful sincerity would enable me to overcome all obstacles in my path. All of these hardships would eventually appear as an illusionary blip, like the static on a screen not quite tuned in. Misunderstanding that might feel, at the moment, like a personal vendetta would later seem like a trivial, temporary obstacle, for people of limited consciousness lack the power to win the battle against the Light force.

I have hardened myself gradually against the challenges of my task, that of carrying the seed of immortality that has already sent its message to tens of thousands of individuals and will undoubtedly touch many more. Just as a seed sometimes has a casing that enables it to survive in inhospitable surroundings but begins to grow through this hardness when it is in a medium that will support it, so Kabbalists of the future may have an easier time. Because now, for the very first time in 3,400 years, the instrument to defy death has been put into motion. Each year since we began our mission, the awareness of people has been raised to another level of consciousness.

TIME TRAVEL

There is nothing to reality aside from consciousness.

Of course, the fact that tomorrow is included in the past is most strikingly illustrated at our Mount Sinai revelation experience.

In our day-to-day lives, a strange paradox exists. Although people are consumed by death consciousness, they are at the same time engaged in an incredible denial of death. It's as if life and death have been reversed. For example, there is rarely an adult who has not been asked to purchase life insurance so as to provide for his or her dependent children in the event of the death of the provider. Ever the questioner, I have wondered, Why do the insurance companies call this "life insurance," when its proper name should be "death insurance," inasmuch as payment of this policy will occur only when the insured dies?

But those who attend our celebration of the revelation on Mount Sinai are truly acquiring life insurance—a guarantee that they will survive for the next three or four months. For the present, this small taste of immortality is a pleasure to offer, just as before a large meal one is offered a sample of the chef's talents in order to whet the appetite.

In the 20 years that the Centre has been providing the Kabbalistic revelation experience, there has not been a single death among those who have attended in the four-month period immediately following the revelation experience. This is what the master had originally foreseen when he shared his vision of mini-immortality. Little did Karen or I know where that humble beginning would take us. Today, thousands of people around the globe are reaping the benefits of the master's prophecy.

The idea that mini-immortality was a virtual

reality spread like wildfire. The notion that a time-travel machine was available has even intrigued scientists. While the Centre's findings could not be verified by conventional scientific methods, this did not deter students from around the world from attending the Mount Sinai revelation experience.

To achieve immortality, albeit for four months only, required traveling back in time. Although the time machine has thus far been a part of science fiction only and not of science, scientists have explained that if such a thing as a time machine ever existed, it would be as if time slowed down in actuality. While the years would go by, in real time, we would not age. When we achieve permanent immortality, the clock stops altogether, for all time.

Although the rational mind cannot grasp the concept of time slowing down or stopping permanently, the fact has already been established. The controversy that has surrounded our claims in this regard may be compared to the 19th century debate over air travel. Some claimed that heavier-than-air machines would never remain aloft yet pioneers persisted until airplanes became a reality.

Time travel simply means that one can travel faster than the speed of light. Albert Einstein claimed that it was impossible to travel faster than the speed of light because if one could, then there would be no past, present, or future. Everything would be in the here and now, the present. Time would stop. There would be no aging. Einstein never proved that one cannot travel faster than the speed of light. He merely reasoned that such a phenomenon could not exist. If it did, people could travel back in time; they would go back and stop upon reaching their vigorous youth.

Einstein did not believe in time travel simply because he did not see the theory in practice. He could not accept the theory of immortality because he could not personally witness this reality. Today science has confirmed that there do exist particles that can travel faster than the speed of light. Science is finally catching up with Kabbalah.

Yet one of the obstacles that science must deal with is their famous uncertainty principle. How aptly it is titled! It demonstrates how far physics remains behind Kabbalah, for as we know, one of the prime causes of chaos is that the Satan has infused human consciousness with the principle of uncertainty. We must choose to change all this.

To achieve temporary or permanent immortality requires certainty that the revelation on Mount Sinai will accomplish this long-sought-after reality. As we stated previously, there is nothing to reality aside from consciousness. If in our minds we have doubts whether the revelation on Mount Sinai creates immortality, then all the Kabbalistic meditations and connections will not serve us in achieving immortality.

This act of traveling back in time was detailed in the Zohar. On the night of the kabbalistic Revelation experience, all those who participate are provided with the methodology that assists them in connecting with the cosmos. It is this vital connection that embodies and perpetuates the energy of mini-immortality.

WATER

Water, water everywhere, and not a drop to drink.

Those familiar words have had little significance for that part of humanity, who never lived in the desert. Unfortunately, these words have taken on a great deal of importance in view of the widespread pollution of our water facilities. The tap water to which we have all become accustomed in most homes or apartments around the globe is now threatened with severe chemical waste that has seeped into our reservoirs and wells. This has prompted a surge in the preference for bottled water—despite the strict tap water regulations enacted by governmental bodies to maintain a standard that is acceptable for human consumption. The fear that has emerged surrounding readily available water has governmental water agencies on the alert, with constant revisions of previous standards that had been established by these very same agencies.

The consciousness that has gripped the public as to the apparent dangers lurking within all drinking water, whether it be tap or bottled, has reached epidemic proportions and has therefore created an unprecedented need for as pure a water as possible. The scandals that have lately surrounded some of the better-known brands of water have become more widespread than ever before. The sales of bottled water are presently at phenomenal and incredible numbers, and growing.

One might have presumed that water, the life blood of human and other forms of life, would be clearly understood by those scientists whose work has led them to the study of its purity. Yet, sorry to say, there is no unanimity by the scientific establishment as to what constitutes purity. We might have assumed that distilled water would be considered as most beneficial for the welfare of the human body, as well as for vegetation, inasmuch as all harmful bacteria is removed from any presence within the water. Yet, strange as it may sound, distilled water is considered to be "dead water," the appropriate scientific name applied to distilled water. While distilled water does not contain any harmful bacteria, at the same time, all beneficial bacteria has likewise been removed, so what is left of this very pure water is, and acts as, a lubricant without any particular benefit to the user of this product. Was this what water was intended for at the time of its creation? Pharmaceutical companies, as required by the FDA, must seek out for their research the purest water in which bacteria will not significantly interfere or alter the results of their research and testing.

Consequently, distilled water has been found to be the most appropriate for scientific research. However, let us remember that its defining feature is still "dead water." The search goes on for water that can meet government standards and still not be considered "dead water." This goal has yet to be reached.

Furthermore, while governmental requirements have established certain standards for water to be considered pure, the meaning of purity has not been clearly defined. When we observe the different labels of bottled water, we will notice that some mention the word "pure" and others do not. What this might indicate at times is that the addition of chlorine or other bacteria-cleansing substances will then permit the manufacturer to label this water as being pure. For the most part, however, the word "pure," as commonly accepted by the consumers of pure water, means that this water meets governmental levels of purity.

From a Kabbalistic perspective, the concept and understanding of pure water goes far and beyond what is generally accepted when the beneficial aspects of water are to be considered. In fact, what matters most to Kabbalist is why water exists in the first place and the purposes and objectives of its presence.

We know there are two elements without which humanity and the universe, with all that it contains, cannot exist: the sun and water. For the purpose of this material, let us examine the character and purpose of water.

What is the internal energy force that causes water to behave as it does? What is known concerning the phenomenon of water is its ability to reject the strong force of gravity. Water will seek its own level, whereas all other elements in the universe, including humans, are subject to and acquiesce to the energy force of gravity, which draws all elements, aside from water, into the bosom of its own character—the internal energy force known as receiving and drawing everything to itself.

In Kabbalistic disciplines, water is considered to possess a sharing energy characteristic, similar to the life-giving force of the Light force of God. The code name used by Kabbalists for water is Chesed. This material essence (water) is the closest that material can portray and symbolize the essence of the Light force of God, which is sharing, and thereby control over all other physical elements of the universe. A rock surrenders to the onslaught of a continuous drop-by-drop of water by ultimately displaying a hole.

So, too, water contains the incredible Light force energy that should and can eliminate all the interferences and obstacles that continue to raise their ugly head within our bodies. So, why do we not experience this very beneficial and therapeutic property of water in our time, or even in the past millenniums of humankind history?

Let us examine the reason behind the apparent inability of water to so dramatically change the health condition of our bodies. Kabbalists ascribed the present condition and character of water to its loss at the time of the Great Deluge. Before the great flood, water, because of its positive Light force character, could not have been used as an instrument to cause chaos and destruction. As a result of extreme human negative activity, which, according to Kabbalah, strongly influences the entire cosmic and physical atmosphere, the healing power of water was removed and, simultaneously, the degeneration of the human body set in.

This might be compared to a pond that becomes stagnant because there is no fresh water to continually cleanse and remove the residue that causes stagnation. Inasmuch as the human body consists of approximately 80 percent water, it stands to reason that the water content exerts an enormous influence and control over the health and welfare of the physical body. Before the Deluge, the purpose of drinking water was to remove any impurities that the body might have accumulated and, therefore, there was extreme longevity for those who lived prior to that time. The water simply flushed and removed any of the obstacles that surfaced within the body. After the Deluge, the power of water no longer could act upon the body and remove accumulated residues. This, consequently, resulted in the aging process and disintegration of the human body. With the loss of water to act as a healing agent, the physician came to describe the onslaught of degeneration that usually begins at age 21.

It has been known to science for quite some time that cells do regenerate every seven years beginning with the date of birth.

At age 7, and at age 126, there is every indication that immortality should continue with a new young body at each seven-year interval.

However, something happens at age 21, when suddenly science recognizes the beginnings of degeneration. The cause for this change in the rejuvenation and regeneration of cells is as yet unknown. Kabbalistically, the reasons for this sudden change in the human body have been well documented, but this is not the place for that matter to be considered.

Because the water that we presently drink does not have the energy to remove whatever obstacles arise at age 21, the immunization structure ultimately becomes deficient. Consequently, because of this immune deficiency, science also has begun to recognize that every physical ailment that the body undergoes during a lifetime is a direct result of a breakdown in the immune system.

If the immune system could undergo a cleansing, both physically and spiritually, then there seems to be no reason why all of the human deficiencies could not again begin to function in a very normal way. If this be the case, then the idea of immortality and how it could be achieved has already been resolved. We simply regenerate every seven years, and the problem of old age simply fades away.

After close to four years studying the possibility of restoring water to its former phase and condition prior to the Great Deluge, it is with great humility that we have merited the information by which we have largely restored water to its proper place in existence. Some 5,000 years have since passed the healing powers of water came to an end. We can only surmise that as a result of the coming of the new millennium in the biblical year of 5760 (2000), the end of chaos has finally arrived.

Inasmuch as we know that the year of the millennium was long ago declared as the year of immortality, whereby the body will no longer undergo the chaos of ill health and death, it would seem very appropriate that restoration of the healing powers within water again reappear at this time.

The restoration of water, along with a cosmos filled with immortality Light force energy, will ultimately and finally bring to a close the pain, suffering, and ill health that have become a part of the human landscape. It is indeed exciting to be a part of this revolutionary and incredible event.

THE SWITCH FOR SINAI IMMORTALITY

"This energy of immortality can always be accessed."
—Rabbi Yehuda Brandwein

The basis of our revelation experience is, of course, the implementation of my master's teachings. I will now finally return to his explanation of exactly how the switch for Sinai immortality can be turned on.

When Light is revealed within the universe, it is destined to remain forever, but the Light remains potential, like electric current in the socket or wall switch. When the appropriate stimulation—in Kabbalistic terminology, a proper vessel—is applied to the Light force, the Light force is reignited and revealed. "Inasmuch as the Light force of immortality on Mount Sinai had once become revealed," explained my master, "this energy of immortality can always be accessed."

Rabbi Luria, in his voluminous work, Gates of Meditation, provided the necessary vessel or switch for Sinai immortality. This procedure could not accomplish the revelation of immortality, however, unless it was applied at the appropriate cosmic time of its original revelation. The guidelines were included within the Biblical code as deciphered by the Zohar. Eternal events are as cosmically scripted as are the appearance of the sun, moon, and all other celestial entities. The constellation of Leo in the heavens does not make its appearance in the wintertime, just as the sign of Capricorn will never appear in the heavens during the summer months.

Glancing into the sky with a high-powered telescope reveals each sign of the Zodiac configured with billions of stars appearing at their usual time of the year. Just as a TV guide is necessary for the viewer to know the exact time of the showing of a favorite program, so, too, does the Bible disclose the exact calendar time when the cosmos is prepared to put on its particular program of events. The moment for the immortality event is the sixth day of the lunar month of Gemini. This is the opportunity for humankind to view and tap the energy of immortality.

Let us continue this analogy with the television. Merely turning on the TV will not permit accessing primetime news at 7:00 p.m. Our sets have the potential ability to provide prime-time news. If I turn the set on at 6:00 p.m. or 8:00 p.m., however, I will not see the prime-time news. Nor can the set access a particular program on anything other than the correct day.

The appropriate time to tune into the awesome energy of immortality, my master said, is in the evening of the sixth day of lunar Gemini. This is the incredible information that only a Zohar can furnish. The entire evening up until, and including, the early morning must be devoted to accessing this unbelievable energy. The body must undergo deprivation. By implementing the codes for accessing immortality provided in detail by Rabbi Isaac Luria, states the

Zohar, every person is guaranteed that he or she shall not die for at least the next four months.

Now when I first heard these words, I had never heard anything like them before. All I could think was, "Too good to be true!" When I shared this reaction with my master, and asked if what he was saying had been proven or substantiated before in history, he answered, "No, that will be your task."

SPEAKING TO THE ANGEL OF DEATH

The secret codes devoted to strengthening the immune system have been recorded by the Kabbalists over the past 2,000 years.

"What do I have to do with this?" I muttered. "How am I going to prove such an outlandish idea, when everything around us stands as evidence that death cannot be avoided or canceled, except when a governor pardons a prisoner and saves him from execution? In the case of a criminal, however, I can understand delaying or canceling an execution. That death was originally in man's hands, as is its negation. But how can one speak to the Angel of Death and tell him to get lost?"

"Furthermore," I asked my master, "if someone does escape death, how can we know it is because of our methods and not because of some other reason?"

"Only wait," said the master, "and sometime in the near future the proof will appear."

If it had been anyone but my master speaking, I would have considered this reply a perfect cop-out. This was the master speaking, however, and as with all master Kabbalists, the concept of yesterday, today, and tomorrow simply does not exist. They were merely repeating what it was their destiny to repeat: the truth. Everything was in the here and now.

The master has revealed to me that the hold the Satan maintains over the cells must be removed through a kind of "metaphysical surgery." This must be accomplished long before the ailment makes its physical appearance. To achieve this feat does not involve destroying the cell. Removing the Light force and its DNA from the cell will release the Satan's hold. When the Light force is surgically removed from the cell or vessel, which is the receptacle for the Light force, the Satan immediately senses that his lifeline and connections to the Light force are no longer channels or carriers for the Light force. He sees no further purpose in remaining connected to the cell and will immediately go looking for other prey. In biochemical terms, we will no longer hold any valence for the Satan.

The aging process sets in only when cells or vessels have become adulterated by our negative consciousness, which creates an affinity with negative entities. This is the cue for the Satan's entrance into our bodies, businesses, and home environments. Once he establishes his hold, all hell breaks loose. The Light force withdraws so as not to fuel the entities with unlimited energy. With each withdrawal, the entities become more aggressive, sensing that their fuel supply is running low, and begin invading other cells.

I would be remiss if I did not devote some ink to the physical realm of activity. The balance between cell, Light force, and the Satan depends upon the dominion of the negative entities over the physical body's repair or immune system. What science is prepared to accept at this critical juncture in medicine is the idea that the immune system is the vital weapon in the battle against all bodily diseases. But science has been unsuccessful is in its attempt to improve the immune system.

The secret codes devoted to strengthening the immune system have been recorded by Kabbalists over the past 2,000 years. Only recently has the meaning of these codes begun filtering into our consciousness. I will deal with this subject in a later book. I know this might be frustrating to many readers who want the information now. However, if we have learned anything from the master's teachings, let us recall how disease and illness emerge. Nothing on an immaterial level evolves instantly. The true solutions to these maladies must also evolve over time.

It is only on the level of gross material reality that "instant" anything prevails—instant pleasure, instant fulfillment, and fast, fast relief. On this illusionary level of reality, however, nothing is permanent. Here today, gone tomorrow. Why? For the profound reason that my master mentioned: the Satan can access us only when we have consciously created negative entities through our thoughts and actions.

We can now begin to understand why immortality is real and mortality is an illusion. Mortality specifies something of an impermanent nature. Immortality is closely associated with an eternal or permanent state of things. How strange that even here, in the common use of these two words, the Satan has kept us away from careful examination. When I mention that immortality is real and mortality is illusionary, my readers' first responses would naturally have been, "What are all those cemeteries about?" and "Where can I observe the reality of immortality?" Why haven't the words themselves aroused us to examine their implication as to what is illusory and what is not?

METAPHYSICAL REMEDIES

I am not a physician or healer,
but I can share the divine knowledge of Kabbalah.

Let me illustrate what I mean by telling you a story of something that happened several years ago. One of our teachers approached me at the revelation event and mentioned that in his center there was a woman who had breast cancer and had begun chemotherapy. He asked me if I would like to talk to her and share some comforting words. "Of course," I replied.

I felt the woman's pain. She knew that she had an enemy within, an enemy that could hide as it went on eating away at her 24 hours a day. She could run and hide and perhaps escape from the enemy without, but she couldn't hide from the enemy within.

During our conversation this woman mentioned that she was due for another chemotherapy treatment a few days following the revelation event. I cautioned her to sit next to her teacher at the event to be certain that she fulfilled all the requirements and secured all the proper meditations and connections. I told her that I was certain that the Light would direct her with the precise recommendation for waging war against this enemy from within. Above all, I told her, maintain a consciousness that the power of immortality will set in within you and then I shall be capable of channeling the right information. "I am not a physician or healer," I told her. "But I can share the divine knowledge of Kabbalah."

During the evening, I received what I believed was a proper approach in dealing spiritually with her medical problem. She was to return to her attending physician and ask him whether she could stop the treatment at this point. She should ask if there would be any adverse effects if she suspended the treatments for three months and then returned to continue them if necessary. In fact I knew that it was unusual for a physician to go along with the idea of discontinuing treatment.

The woman returned from the revelation event with a consciousness that the immortality energy intelligence had indeed embraced her entire body. What this meant to her and to all the participants was that the peculiar force that the Zohar labels as the core and origin of death had been removed. In contrast to medicine's notion that people die of various diseases and ailments, the Zohar classifies these supposed causes of death as only symptoms. Heart and lung failure, cirrhosis of the liver, and other so-called fatal diseases are merely extensions and expressions of the death force. Remove the seed of death—the worm, as the Zohar designates this force—and one has erased the traces of death from his or her body.

The woman returned home, and the following day went for her appointment with the oncologist. To her amazement, the physician agreed to her request to discontinue chemotherapy and told her to return for periodic checkups.

We then commenced with the program of Kabbalistic surgery, which she agreed to follow strictly and without hesitation. I again cautioned her to maintain the consciousness of immortality to ensure that the powerful tool of mind over matter would at no time leave her body. There could be no doubt that this segment of the treatment was the most difficult. I repeated something that she had heard over and over again as a student of the Centre: We are completely responsible for the death force invading our bodies. Our negative activity and behavior toward others and our inability to maintain a vigil of positive consciousness contributes to the break in our natural, God-given security shield. Once the Satan senses the rupture in our security cover, he swoops down, penetrating us with the death force.

Unfortunately, the only disease that we recognize as an invader of the body is cancer. The patient's heightened fear breaks down the immune system. Fear aggravates the mind, and this anxiety, in turn, feeds the cancer cell, thus beginning revolving state of panic that spreads the cancer. Our consciousness fails to understand that all serious diseases that can lead to ultimate death are of Satanic design. The victim is unaware of the infiltrator. This is precisely what medical science is referring to when it says that a disease began long before its physical manifestation. However, no medical therapy or device can approach a disease in its infancy or metaphysical state and presence. This is precisely the level that Kabbalah addresses.

We provided our student, the woman with breast cancer, with the methodology to battle the enemy within. With the aid of a visual schema to direct the Light force toward the origin of the breast cancer, as well as other techniques of supportive therapy, she has remained free and clean of the death forces that once claimed her.

At one time this student called me to report that she had some discomfort, not pain, in her breast. I asked her if uncertainty had somehow crept into her consciousness. She told me that she had a friend with a similar condition and this had awakened some fear within her. I assured her that the discomfort would disappear with her fear.

I reminded her that while the immortality event

and the follow-up by Kabbalistic treatment had removed the negative entities from her body, this did not mean that the Satan had been eliminated. He was gone from her body, yes, but as long as immortality is not firmly entrenched, the Satan lurks, seeking an opening or breach in our security shields. He is ever on the lookout for the opportunity to swoop down upon his unsuspecting victims and assault them with his chaos.

THE BIG QUESTION

Why do any cells become what they become?

The Zohar views the Bible as the coded blueprint of the universe and the road map for people to achieve control over their destiny. To the average reader of the Bible, its contents have remained concealed for the past 3,400 years. Even with the deciphering of the biblical codes by the Zohar 2,000 years ago, not until the 20th century was the possibility of comprehending the contents of the Zohar given to the people. Now the Kabbalah Centre provides a peek into the ancient vault. Recall that this battleground between the Light force and the Satan—code words for the positive and the negative—is non-material and thus undetectable. Without Kabbalah, the battle between these forces takes 30, 40, or more years. As the battle rages without benefit of the positive entities Kabbalah provides, the Light force continues to remove itself. DNA, the factory for building and rebuilding the body, receives its fuel and instructions from the Light force. With the gradual reduction of the Light force's presence, DNA gradually slows down repair and replacement.

Everyone knows about the gradual withdrawal of the Light force, and everyone is in agreement that this happens. What is new in this picture is the revelation, given by my master, that Kabbalah changes this process. My master imparted this astonishing information to me in a light manner, asking, with a little laughter, why the scientists haven't asked how the cells know, when they are in an undifferentiated state of existence, which one becomes a heart and which one a lung. Why do any cells become what they become? The answer, my master told me, is the intelligence energy of the Light force.

AWARENESS OF THE EXISTENCE OF THE FIRST BODY

One body is visible, and one is invisible.

There will be those who reject anything that lacks evidence, my master told me, but he explained that the information has been with us a very long time. The evidence will be forthcoming in the 21st century.

"Please tell the readers just to have an open mind so the information can be drawn in," said my master. "Mankind has for too long had a closed mind and has thereby prevented the revelation of this wonderful age of new phenomena. When thoughts such as these are expressed, it is only a matter of time before the empirical evidence appears."

He then went on to explain the heart of the matter regarding the true existence of two bodies—one visible, one invisible—where we generally acknowledge the existence of only one, ignorant of God's truth. As an illustration he employed the story of Elijah.

Elijah the prophet, declares Scripture, flew straight to heaven. He did not undergo a funeral. The Zohar interprets this event by saying that Elijah never died. Elijah's return to the physical realm is recognized in two ways. The first is the requirement of Elijah's presence at every circumcision in order for the ceremony to be binding and beneficial. Forgetting to openly and verbally invite Elijah is considered a serious failure. Elijah is also extended an invitation to the Passover Seder, when a cup of wine is specially set out for him and the door is opened for him to enter.

"According to the Zohar," the master explained, "Elijah had two bodies—one remained on earth and the other was his vehicle among the celestial angels."

HOW OUR EVERYDAY BODIES RENEW THEMSELVES EVERY SEVEN YEARS

"The first, translucent body is attained by the righteous person,
and it is instrumental in maintaining the outer body."
—*Rabbi Yehuda Brandwein*

"What the Zohar reveals for us," he continued, "is a duality that exists in the human body. There is the outer or external body that we are all familiar with. We will refer to it as the second body for it is impermanent in comparison to the inner, first body, which can only be observed and revealed to those individuals with an elevated state of consciousness. The first, translucent body is attained by the righteous person, and it is instrumental in maintaining the outer body. It does not decompose in the grave. It is within this first, translucent body that Elijah appeared among the angels."

"Sounds like the astronauts to me," I exclaimed. "They need a second set of clothes to walk among the stars."

My master did not miss a beat. "This dramatic Zohar," he explained, "will illuminate the mysteries surrounding immortality/restoration in general and the questions you have raised, including the big one. You see, it is the cells of the outer body—the second body—that undergo a rejuvenation by returning back to an undifferentiated state of existence. But the first, translucent body is one that the Satan cannot bond with. This body is constantly present and sustains the individual at all times and, more specifically, when the outer body undergoes a transformation from differentiated cell to undifferentiated one."

"When the outer body returns for its rejuvenation back to the embryonic state of existence, the eternal body supports the ongoing internal life system, just as an iron lung breathes for a patient. While this is taking place, neither the individual nor the observer notice any change going on. It is so subtle that not even the Satan understands what is happening. the Satan assumes that he remains bonded to the cell when, in fact, the cell with its dual life has, through the action of the Creator, momentarily returned for a turning back of its clock. Thus it becomes a reborn cell. This is one of those moments when the master magician, the Satan, has a beautiful trick played on him by the Creator himself. The heart and lung of the internal translucent body keep the 'fort' intact, while the outer body has gone for its seven-year return to the fountain of youth."

This information really excited me. For the first time, I understood why immortality is the real thing and mortality is what appears to be the essence of reality. The first body never dies, but most of us never even know it is there. We do not see it and, therefore, for us, it doesn't exist. Paradoxically, the second body, the one we all see and observe, is the one that everyone regards as dying.

The Satan has us all believing that there is nothing out there except what we can feel and touch, despite the fact that everything that is visible is here today and gone tomorrow.

WITHIN THE GRIP OF MORTALITY

The Light force DNA must bow to a person's free will.

So let us examine the consequence of our new understanding. Why, after "death," does the DNA not continue to reproduce new cells every seven years? We know the fingernails and hair continue to grow. If the whole body continued its renewal, we could maintain our youth and enjoy immortality.

The answer is simple. The world's consciousness is bound to the belief in mortality and therefore, we cannot break the Satan's hold over the cells. They are prisoners of the Satan and, after "death," cannot return to an embryonic state of rejuvenation. The aging process occurs because the Light force DNA is required to withdraw further and further as the Satan continues his unrestricted march across our bodies. The aging problems remain as long as we do not apply the newly revealed secrets of the universe, which can force Satan to withdraw from the human battlefield. The Light force DNA is ever present to fire up newly rejuvenated, undifferentiated cells. Let us assume, however, that the person is dominated by the desire to receive for the self alone. In this case, the Light force DNA, which is always in our bodies and does not leave even after "death," must bow to the free will of the person, and must withdraw or withdraw the desire to share.

"This universal law," claimed the master, "is what underlies chaos. Consider the rejuvenation of cells in a person who chooses to engage in negative thinking. While such a person often feels sorry for himself and thinks his bad thoughts of others do not reflect on himself, the true situation is quite different. By having these negative thoughts, the person has unwittingly invited negative entities into his most private domain, his own body. The person has broken the natural, healing, protective shield surrounding the body and has opened the door for the Satan to make his grand entrance. Upon entrance, the host of Satan's subordinates, those whose specialties are the heart, lung, and all other parts of our bodies, are all invited to participate in the festivities of breakfast, lunch, and dinner — all day, all night, all year, for as long as the food lasts. The food, unfortunately, is our bodies, our business, our social lives, our family environments. The food will last only as long as the body lasts."

Mortality is a dirty trick played upon the Satan and, unfortunately, on all those who are left behind. The Satan is not prepared for this abrupt ending. Whether he devours one cell or the entire body, which results in death, the Satan is disappointed about the food running out. After one cell, the Satan must go after another and another, until he runs out of cells. Then he has a rude awakening: his own greed, his own desire to receive for the self alone—similar to that of human negative consciousness—damages him.

SHARING AND ACCOUNTABILITY

"We and we alone are responsible."
—*Rabbi Yehuda Brandwein*

"But, God," some will ask, "where are you when I need you most?" God is right here. Unfortunately, we shackled the Light force DNA when we opted for negativity. We said to the Light force DNA, "Look here, I'm not into this sharing idea like you, Light force DNA. I've got to do my thing. I've decided to follow the path and rules of the Satan. But hang out. Maybe tomorrow I'll have time for you and some sharing."

"The conclusion we must come to from all this," said the master, "is that we and we alone are responsible for our chaos, pain, and suffering. It becomes quite obvious that refraining from negative consciousness and negative activity is not merely a question of morals and ethics. What it comes right down to is that it simply isn't advisable. It is not in our best interest. In fact, negative thoughts and activities have been determined to be harmful to our health and may cause mortality."

KABBALAH KNOWLEDGE IS ESSENTIAL TO OUR WELL-BEING

The reader might be wondering why Kabbalah knowledge is essential to our well-being, in every aspect of our lives. Well, knowledge is not, as most people believe, a means to an end. Knowledge is an end in itself. Not just its use but its sheer presence is an integral part of therapeutic remedies, an essential link in the chain that promises to connect with the ultimate goal of immortality.

THE AGE OF INFORMATION: KNOWLEDGE AND IMMORTALITY

The Light force will no longer remain as a passive force.

The Zohar confirms that what will distinguish the age of information will be an infusion of the Light force into our cosmos. The Light force will literally invade our space with knowledge and power, to an extent unknown since the two other "big moments" of immortality: the moment of the Garden of Eden and the all-too-brief 40 days at the time of the Exodus. The third moment—the moment for my contribution—has come.

When I fathomed this level of the Zohar, I asked the master, "What does all this mean?"

His response was one of joy and sadness at the same time. "In this age of information, the Light force has made its intentions clear to the world. It will no longer remain a passive force to be called upon when the need arises. The consciousness of humankind has been raised. This has become increasingly evident by the radical changes that have made the scientific world dynamic on an unprecedented scale. The outpouring of knowledge within the scientific community in the past 70 years has surpassed the significance of what had been discovered by science in the previous 2,000 years!

"The same 70 years have given birth to Kabbalistic knowledge and information never before accessible to the people, including people previously unacquainted with any form of Biblical studies. As never before in history, people have begun to assume control over their daily lives. Rather than surrender to the scripts of others, people have begun to express their desires. There will be more individualistic activity and less central, governmental, and organizational control."

THE PEOPLE AND THE MYSTERIES OF KABBALAH

*Extraordinarily difficult challenges
will pass into the realm of the possible.*

This, the master told me, is both good and bad. On the one hand, spiritual-minded people will begin to reveal the hidden secrets of immortality and restoration as a result of the massive infusion of the Light force. Things that could not be observed and noticed just a few short years ago will have their veils removed merely by our consciousness that the impossible is possible. Eventually, extraordinarily difficult challenges will pass into the realm of the possible, such as restoration of lost body parts and even resurrection of the dead—in short, immortality.

People with ill intentions will also make use of this power, the master warned. They will make every attempt to disrupt moves toward a life free of chaos and despair, but they will be powerful only to the extent that the kind and righteous people are weak.

An expanded awareness and elevated consciousness, states the Zohar, are the legacy of Kabbalah in this age of information. It is simply a matter of disengaging from the darkness of the Satan consciousness and illusion and becoming consciously connected with the reality of the Light of the Creator. Rabbi

Azulai has repeatedly stated that the resurrection or the restoration of body parts requires only the raising of our consciousness in the extraordinary and miraculous period in which we are living.

THE LIMITS OF SCIENCE

People will no longer settle for living in a state of chaos.

The most advanced computer that man will ever perfect will contain an infinite number of calculations. Yet this is the number of eternity, of the Creation of God. Although science has come closer and closer to grappling with the mysteries of infinite space and time, due to this limitation, science will have to eventually back off from its grandiose plan. More and more, it will be giving us explanations that will lead us away from the truth and reality.

Yet people will no longer settle for living within a state of fragmentation and chaos. They are tired of this approach. Humanity's battle with the negative forces is drawing to a close, and there is no going back to our previous ways.

Because we are now experiencing an extraordinary infusion of Light force energy into our cosmos, the paradoxical situation foreseen in the Zohar is already in full force. With all the advanced research in medicine taking place around the globe, cancer and a host of other illnesses and disabilities are still uncontrollable. Furthermore, new viruses, unknown only a decade or two ago, have come to the fore. Additionally, diseases considered extinct, refuse to leave us. Some, such as smallpox, are even being intentionally kept alive by those who are thinking of germ warfare—still in the grip of the Satan's plan to foment conflict among humanity. Medicine and science alone are clearly unequal to the task of bringing about peace and the ultimate well-being of the earth's inhabitants.

THE ULTIMATE BATTLE

*"We have come to a point in time
where the old rules go out the window."*
—*Rabbi Yehuda Brandwein*

Dear reader, I dare to be a heretic of hope. I dare to say that humanity shall win the battle against the Satan's forces and achieve connection with the infinite spiritual force just as, at the conclusion of many a protracted war, often the final battles are the most brutal ones, for each side realizes what is at stake.

The Light force is increasing the Satan's fuel supply. For this reason, the suffering of afflicted persons is increasing, despite the invention of new pain killers. If left unchecked, the Satan and his horde of viruses and bacteria will run rampant, and the biological warfare we see in the movies will become reality. Woe unto those who would live in such a period.

We do not, however, have to live that way. We can turn instead to the Zohar, which says, "Praiseworthy are those who shall know how to maintain control over the evil forces that can devour others." Just within the past year or two, thousands of people who have already turned to the Zohar have testified to the difference that knowing the secrets of the universe has made in their lives.

This reminds me that I do not want to leave the reader with the impression that the battle between the forces of good and evil is only operative on the level of the human body and its health or illness. In fact, as the final battle intensifies, confusion and frustration will also reign in the financial community. This chaos will bring about crises in the global economy, an increase in warfare, and the instability of governments.

Many people have already become aware that markets are now much more volatile than they once were. The swings of the stock markets and the erratic fluctuation of currencies are topics that my master asked me to discuss. He asked me to present a picture of economic circumstances that would be unpredictable by even the most noted economists. "We have come to a point in time," said my master, "where the old rules go out the window." With each passing day the financial markets have acted more like the ball in a ping-pong match.

"We are coming to understand," explained my master, "that it is not physical reality that can or cannot establish certainty or uncertainty in our times. Fluctuations within the physical, material realm are first determined on the metaphysical or immaterial level of consciousness."

Although the Light force helps us gain control over our lives, let us remember that control refers to one aspect and one aspect alone. Despite the extraordinary influence of the Light force in the cosmos when the heavenly gates are opened, if the Satan has not been defeated he will tap into what will be an infinite source of energy to fuel chaos. Much is at stake.

THE END OF DAYS AND IMMORTALITY

Yes, we can have our cake and eat it, too!

In Kabbalistic doctrine, the End of Days, which is our current era, will include a final deathblow to the negative energy of the physical body, thus bringing about the demise of the Angel of Death himself.

This event can be realized through spiritual development on an individual basis, and also globally, when a critical mass of spiritual transformation and enlightenment is achieved among the earth's inhabitants.

This deathblow can occur symbolically through proactive spiritual growth and the complete subjugation of the ego. Or, it can occur through the pain and suffering associated with physical death, in a doom-and-gloom, fire-and-brimstone conclusion to the drama of physical human existence.

However we might achieve transformation, once our soul's desire to share—our true essence inherited from our Creator—is free to blossom unencumbered by the body's self-indulgent impulses, it will pave the way for the emergence of immortality.

Humans will then be in a position to reconcile the two intelligences of receiving and sharing, giving birth to a new dynamic perfectly aligned with the sharing attribute of the Creator.

Referring to this unique metamorphosis, my teacher's master, Rabbi Ashlag wrote, "The body, together with its extensive desire to receive, will no longer be able to cause us harm. On the contrary, we shall take control of it, and we shall give it the form of sharing."

A simple story illustrates this simple yet profound idea: Rachel has been on a strict diet for many months. She has lost over 20 pounds and continues to do very well. One day, her closest friend Deborah invites her over for dinner. Knowing how much Rachel loves Black Forest cake, Deborah spends the entire day lovingly baking her the most wonderful cake. Meanwhile, Rachel has successfully shut down all her desires to cheat throughout the course of her diet. One piece of cake at this time will definitely not spoil or undermine her effort, but Rachel remains determined not to cheat when she arrives at her best friend's home for dinner.

After the meal, Deborah surprises Rachel with her deliciously decadent desert. It's obvious how much love and effort was put into baking the cake. Rachel realizes that she must accept a piece in order to share with her best friend.

In other words, Rachel receives for the sake of sharing with Deborah. In turn, Rachel is rewarded with a wonderful piece of cake, and Deborah receives untold pleasure by sharing with Rachel. The act of sharing becomes a circular, and thus, eternal concept with both people bestowing pleasure to one another.

When humanity has collectively removed all selfish desires and negative urges from its nature, the "sharing gene" inherited from the Light of the Creator will be free to bloom. Then our desire to receive will be able to take on the form of sharing, because we will now know how to receive endless pleasure, not for our own sakes, but for the sake of sharing with the Creator. Yes, we can have our cake and eat it, too!

As Rabbi Ashlag so profoundly points out in his writings, nothing in the world makes the Creator happier then bestowing pleasure upon His creation.

Humanity will have attained the sharing nature of the Light, bringing us in perfect unity with the Light of the Creator.

For the individual who proactively completes this spiritual work before a critical mass is met, immortality means that the curtain of illusion will be pulled back and the supernal mysteries of life will be understood with exquisite clarity. It means peace of mind, the removal of chaos from our personal lives, and a rapid gearing down of the aging process. It will offer immunity against the negative forces that bring about decay and deterioration in our relationships, our prosperity, and our emotional well-being.

Once this negative death force is eliminated from our life, we're free to attract opportunities, people, and events that overflow with positive energy. In other words, Murphy's Law is repealed, so that whatever can possibly go right in our lives will go right. The Garden of Eden will not be a long-sought-after paradise located in some remote island in the world to come, but a state of mind that we experience in the here and now. This sacred quality of life will be the norm until global immortality is attained.

Our total certainty and conviction in these spiritual truths will accelerate the process of transformation, and the signs of change will become very apparent on a practical, physical level.

OPENING THE MIND TO THE OPEN GATES

We require a complete revolution in understanding.

If all is in order—if complete certainty has been established and conditions are in harmony with the dictates of the Zohar—the aging process will be reversed. This could come about shortly. The success of that third moment will depend upon two things.

The Light force must determine that the heavenly gates of the cosmos become opened and the secrets of restoration immortality can fill our consciousness. The second criterion is that the level of human consciousness is sufficiently high. This depends upon how well we can open ourselves to radically new ideas.

Some of you might wonder why I mention "heavenly gates," a term used by religionists. The answer is critical. When we were children, we would read about these pearly gates and how, if we were good, we would enter them. At that time we did not realize that scientists would, in fact, discover gates in the celestial realm now known as the "Van Allen belts." We did not know that the entire space program would be dependent upon when these gates were open or shut. This concept, like so many other current developments, was anticipated by the Zohar when Rabbi Shimon provided the timetables dictating when the gates were to be opened for the extraordinary infusion of the Light force into the celestial and terrestrial realm. Yet again, we are reminded of how far science has to go to begin to catch up with the sublime wisdom of Kabbalah.

The case that I have made for the entrance of restoration of immortality onto the stage of human history rests on the dates provided by Kabbalists. Science has corroborated the dramatic influence of this age of information by accepting the exciting possibilities of bioengineering, genetic decodification projects, and cloning. However, to get people to accept the reality of immortality is a task that will require a complete revolution in understanding. This requires an understanding of how mortality has come to so dominate our consciousness until this point in human history. I hope that this volume is a valuable contribution to achieving that understanding on a global scale.

SECTION V

THE MILLENNIUM

A GREAT COSMIC MOMENT

A new millennium is a cosmic event that crosses the calendar every one thousand years. Numerous systems have been devised to keep track of the passage of years. One of the oldest in continuous use is the Biblical reckoning of time. The Bible starts the reckoning of time with the end of the seventh day of creation. The time prior to that could have covered a period of trillions of years. These are not included in the Biblical calendar. Thus, the first millennium occurred approximately 5,753 years ago, according to the biblical calendar.

Each millennium is freighted with enormous and profound historical symbolism. The millennium is basically a cosmic event where a 1,000-year epoch yields to another. A great cosmic moment. A millennial year has occurred only five times, when counting is based on the idea of original Biblical creation. The Kabbalah assigns a Sfirah (a specific dimension of the Light force) to each of the millennial years. The sixth millennium is the Sfirah, Yesod.

Therefore, there is an undeniable consciousness that permeates and reverberates around the globe with each passing millennium. Time is mysterious and elastic, although it is the organizing principle of conscious human effort. We organize our lives by the clock and appointment books. Yet little do we realize that time, while elastic, nevertheless is our chance to see, or to imagine that we see, history's narrative framework. Delineated time is the way to make sense out of beginnings, in between, and the finale.

The Christian millennium year of 2000 is recently upon us. While this millennial date is an arbitrary mark on the calendar, people already have begun to wonder what the new frontier beyond 2000 will be, what the future will look like after that moment. Millennial expectations and predictions have already appeared all around the globe.

According to biblical reckoning, the year 2000 began during the Hebrew calendar year 5760. On the surface, the year 5760 doesn't impress us with having any deep significance, certainly nothing close to the excitement expressed about the 2,000-year millennium, when party lovers around the globe booked rooms, made reservations, and devised plans for the mega-night.

Where science and technology once offered a future of the fulfillment of dreams, today the future is seen as problematic. The new millennium brought with it an increasing skeptical attitude toward science and a renewed attraction to spiritual values as opposed to material gratification and human excesses.

In recent years the slowly escalating threats of a nuclear nightmare, the vanishing ozone, overpopulation, world hunger, and plagues such as AIDS have appeared as the last millennium came to a close. Perhaps our thought and consciousness require a threat of doom to shake us loose from the doldrums that have brought us to this dangerous moment in history.

Whether these catastrophic implications will indeed bring humankind to a rude awakening still remains to be seen. For whatever reason, people have the inclination to jump into the fire rather than flee from it. This has been the steady and continuous landscape that we have created for ourselves. It therefore is refreshing to refer to an incredible section among the numerous writings of the famed and sainted Kabbalist, Rabbi Avraham Azulai, and realize that despite our headlong desire to rush into a disastrous situation, this scenario may actually come to a pleasant ending.

Furthermore, the predictions that we shall shortly merit the opportunity to reverse the aging process, restore limbs, and experience similar miraculous events are no longer in the category of "pie in the sky," although a reaction of skepticism may be expected. Murphy's Law remains the centerpiece of Jewish consciousness. This is understandable considering the past 2,000 years of Jewish history.

I have always questioned Murphy's Law. Why not create a new law that states, "If anything can go right, it will." Does this notion seem to be so outrageous or absurd? The answer lies in the fact that we are influenced by the laws of the Tree of Knowledge of Good and Evil whose commander-in-chief is the Dark Lord.

However, when we abandon the Tree of Knowledge reality, we will shift into high gear and connect with the awesome power of the Tree of Life universe where fragmentation, time zones, and chaos do not exist. There are no openings within this atmosphere where the Dark Lord can enter; consequently things cannot go wrong.

When something seems to have gone wrong within the Tree of Life reality, this is nothing more than a test of our reaction. Do we really believe in the Light force's ability to maintain order in our lives? Or do we retain our belief in the Light force of the Lord only when things go our way, as if we really know what is good for us?

The chances that a change may come over the consciousness of the Jewish people are indeed slim. Therefore the Jew is always under pressure from without to undergo changes, even if that means "running from place to place." However, due to the cosmic influence of the Aquarian age, changes in consciousness have already begun. This is further substantiated by Rabbi Avraham Azulai in his volume, *Chesed L'Avraham*.

THE POWER OF WATER

There is a transmission in our possession from the Kabbalists that there are 400 groups of chaotic bundles of energy (Tumah). And to remove these groups from their internal energy force requires 40 s'ah (a measure of volume for dry objects and for liquids). And each s'ah contains or holds 144 average-sized eggs. Thus 40 s'ah comes to 5,760.

And since a human being is structured or put together from the four elements (water, fire, air and earth), the cleansing of any and all impurities (illness, plagues, mental disease) is by virtue of the energy intelligence of water. The reason for this is that Spirit, the force energizing these impurities, is what must be removed and not merely the impurity stated in scriptures, "And the Spirit of the unclean shall I remove from the earth." And the force behind these unclean groups, whose internal nature is never to enter or come in contact with (the force of) water, when the impurity enters or becomes submerged in water, the spirit energizer is removed from the impurified entity.

Therefore the Sages required that an unclean person completely immerse the entire body; that even if one hair of the head remains above and outside the water, the impurity remains. The reason being that whatever group of negative forces have taken hold on the individual, when these impure forces flee from the water and they can still attach themselves to some part of the body, be it only a strand of hair, when the rest of the body leaves the haven of water refuge, the evil forces then return and dwell in the rest of the body.

According to the innermost secrets of the internal nature of water, the uppermost energy intelligence, Chesed (mercy), is the awesome power of water's effectiveness to remove and purify any blemish or impurity. As stated in scriptures, "Chesed (mercy) and truth shall erase inequity."

And the waters of Chesed are drawn from the attribute and Sfirot consciousness (dimension) of Chokhmah (wisdom). The letter Yud of the Tetragrammaton hints at the Sfirot consciousness of Chokhmah. The form of the letter Yud is like the shape and form of an egg. The three letters that comprise the spelling of the name of the letter Yud—Yud Vav Dalet—has a numerical value of 144. How do we arrive at the sum value of 144?

a) The six varied combinations of the three letters

that spell out the sound letter of Yud. Numerically, these six combinations add up to 120.

b) Add the 18 letters of the six combinations of the letter Yud.

c) The six varied combinations. Together the letter Yud comprises the energy force of the value of 144.

Thus the letter Yud and the s'ah both embody the energy intelligence of the value of 144. Consequently, the Yud, as the s'ah with its measurement, is capable of removing 10 groups of the spirit of Tumah (negative packets of energy). And when 40 s'ah of water combine in a unified whole, they remove from the individual the entire 400 groups of Tumah.

This idea also reveals the secret of the "400 men of Esau" by the Zohar. Also, recognize that at ten specific areas in the body, there are gates or entrances by which the ten general groups of Tumah infiltrate the body and cause disintegration of the internal and external wellbeing of the individual.

1. The first gate is at the head.
2. Jaw or cheek on the right side.
3. Jaw or cheek on the left side. These three gate ways also symbolize the three upper Sfirot (dimensions) of Keter (crown), Chokhmah (wisdom), and Binah (intelligence).

4. The right armpit.
5. The left armpit.
6. The region where there is hair on the throat and on the heart, hinting at the body or trunk of a tree.
7. The right thigh.
8. The left thigh.
9. The area of the sex organ.
10. The buttocks area.

These ten regions act like a throne to the ten groups of Tumah, wherein these negative energy packets become manifest when an individual "becomes Tamei (a spiritual short-circuit)." And know that the required measurement for the Mikveh (a ritual bath to remove negative forces) is 5,760 average-sized eggs.

The secret of this matter is as follows: at the end of the year 5,760, according to the calendar marking (Biblical) creation, the following verse shall become actualized: "And the Spirit (force) of Tumah [400 groups of negative energy forces] shall I remove from this earth." In addition, the verse, "I will rid the land from dangerous animals," referring to the spirit of Tumah as interpreted by the Zohar, shall also become actualized.

A further secret concerning this matter is that the resurrection of the dead will take place in three stages at three different intervals. The first will be the resurrection of those who are Israelites, buried in Israel. The second refers to those Israelites outside of Israel. Finally, the third is the resurrection of the 70 nations. These periods will be times of intense and great judgment. And the third resurrection will take place at the end of the year 5,760 according to the Biblical calendar.

The preceding revelation speaks for itself. The idea of resurrection or restoring limbs now only awaits the raising of our consciousness toward this miraculous period. The notion that we shall retrieve our youth should come as no surprise. Those of us stubborn enough to cling to the present ideas of degeneration and disintegration will unfortunately fall prey to the effects of the harsh judgment days that lie ahead of us.

The lengthy discourse by Rabbi Azulai centers around the concept of the Mikveh, containing the awesome power to remove the origin and essence of all negative groups of energy. While the subject matter of this book does not include this awe-inspiring vehicle for channeling the highest degree of the Light force, nevertheless I feel it appropriate to mention the mystery surrounding the circumstances that brought on an ecstasy of intensity to the sainted Rabbi Ashlag.

When Rabbi Ashlag achieved a "complete separation from corporeality," he literally visualized and saw the cleansing process in operation. He actually saw the water energy-intelligence of the Mikveh charge forward towards the spirits of the Tumah. Terrified, these negative forces began to flee in retreat toward the "last bastion of hair" not yet immersed within the water.

And when the entire body, including the hair, became enveloped and surrounded by the energy intelligence of the water, these negative spirits were left with no alternative but to release their hold on the body. They were forced to let go. They no longer could rely on this particular body for their energy sustenance. The physical domain represented by those abnormal or dark spots in and around the body were completely overrun by the Light force of the Lord. The camps and bases in which these, negative, forces resided were now occupied by the Light force fleet of the Lord. They were outnumbered.

The required sum and quantity of the troops necessary to remove the enemy was present within the ritually correct water of the dimension of 5,760 average-sized eggs. The Dark Lord had no choice but to summon and command his subordinates to completely withdraw from their previously held positions. They were in full retreat. The forces of the Lord began to reoccupy the former locations of their opponents. At long last they were now positioning for the final "mopping-up operations" of the enemy residue left over. The positions were noted and addressed.

Over a period of time, or as long as it would take, the remaining scars and residual trapping left behind by the enemy would be removed and existing usable tissue repaired and transformed into healthy bastions for rejuvenation of the body and mind.

A front-line view of the preceding scenario was granted to Rabbi Ashlag. The metaphysical barriers and curtains were removed on stage to provide a premiere seat for this incredible battle set within the human body. With access to such a premiere, it is little wonder that Rabbi Ashlag sensed euphoria.

We too, all of humankind, are about to witness the greatest event ever presented on the stage of history. Rabbi Azulai and his discourse shall capture the imagination of all of those seeking a fuller and much richer life. The future of humankind hangs in no small measure on the actualization of his prophecy.

The concept of Mikveh gleaned from the dissertation of Rabbi Azulai considers the matter of death and aging as a mystery we often asked about as children, were denied in youth, and reluctantly came to accept as adults. It is considered unlikely or nearly impossible that any of us could live to be 120 years old. Even with the best care it appears that we must grow infirm and subsequently die. While aging is accepted as an obvious fact of life, the causes that contribute to it are not known.

Biological repair systems abound within our physical machine, the body. We are in a constant process of repair, unconsciously or otherwise, from molecules to tissues, or growing our second set of teeth—elephants, six sets, and sharks, an indefinite number during their lifetime. The most visible example of repair to our bodies is wound healing by which we repair damage to our skin or nails.

Regular replacement goes on all the time at the molecular level. Our proteins are provided with a continuous turnover at a rate characteristic of each unique protein. All linings of our intestines are replaced every few days while those lining our urinary bladder once every two months or so.

At the unperceived molecular level, our genetic material, DNA, is regularly undergoing a repair of some sort. There are enzymes that restore and repair damaged bases within the DNA and ignore healthy DNA. Hence while nature is taking us apart, it nevertheless makes every effort to put us back together again daily.

Since some animals, like lizards and starfish, can regenerate severed tails, why doesn't the human body undergo this kind of damage control? What prevents us from having lost teeth replaced, like the shark does? Is there any reason why the joints of arthritic sufferers are not replaced as crabs do? Why, for that matter, are we subject to the many facets of heart disease, rather than continuous repair?

The answer surely has something to do with the evolutionary process dictated by the cosmic calendar. Medical researchers no longer attribute the higher life expectancy to advanced medical technology. The rapid rise in aging is directly related to the influence of the Aquarian age. To suggest a biological changeover from a normal degenerative process due to aging to one of regeneration is exactly what Rabbi Azulai is considering.

The biological repair mechanisms seem to be limited only because aging may be thought of as simply irreparable damage or deterioration. We are consciously or unconsciously preparing ourselves for aging and death. Therefore, Rabbi Azulai found it necessary some 400 years ago to reveal specific dates when we can expect resurrection and restoration. Consequently, with this revealed knowledge, we will hasten the fountain of youth and observe medical history change before our very eyes.

Based on current experiments, a number of scientists are theorizing that within a generation or two humankind's life span could be extended by decades if not by centuries. Why? By altering genes, they believe it may be possible to extend and prolong our life. This notion of a dramatic extension of human life arouses healthy skepticism. After many years of confident forecasts, there is still no cure for cancer.

However, could they possibly be right? The question has to be taken seriously, but not for the same reasons. A series of discoveries about genes that extend the life of simple organisms, and genes that cut it short, could raise hopes for advancing life expectancy. However, from a Kabbalistic perspective, no matter what the outcome of these new aging experiments, the final determiner will be the cosmos.

When the moment comes, the aging process will be reversed. This may come about shortly, as stated by Rabbi Azulai. However long the process may take, one thing remains certain: The days of aging and degeneration are numbered. The time factor depends completely upon our awareness and consciousness. The consciousness and awareness that the resurrection of limbs and bodies is a natural function are necessary for its fruition. With this ingredient Rabbi Azulai's predictions will happen. All physical manifestations of the body are preceded by a stimulus, voluntary or involuntary, and these stimuli are strongly influenced by our belief system.

Researchers, who are now asserting that people can live for many centuries, with scientific evidence to prove it, neglect the element of consciousness. Why now and not two centuries earlier? We, including the scientists, must forego our egos and raise our awareness. We must all come to the inevitable conclusion that cosmic awareness and consciousness are responsible for any successful research and development. But how can cosmic consciousness and awareness come about? And here is where the knowledge of Kabbalah paves the way toward the ultimate goal of "complete resurrection." The answer, fortunately or unfortunately, lies with the people, with humankind.

Is a plague a curse or an opportunity to remove the plague? Are epidemics signs of punishment from the Lord or an event to raise our awareness of the need to eliminate the problem? The sole reason for progress has been the consciousness that problems must and will be solved. The problem of aging will disappear when humankind concludes that there is no valid reason for it being there in the first place.

From time to time, a true genius emerges. Albert Einstein was such a man, the perfect innate consciousness. Einstein, like all true geniuses, was born with a capacity for cosmic connection. Unlike spiritual-seeking individuals, he did not have to strive for connection, he already had it. But the questions that must be raised are:

Did he reveal something that had already existed? Or did he invent something new?

Have Einstein's fellow scientists, by exploring the structure of the universe and devising new hi-sci-tech tools and devices, radically altered the state of existence? No. A genius, far from being the initiator of new concepts and inventions, as commonly believed, is actually a channel for the cosmic unity.

This intellectual energy, in truth, is not entirely the product of the individual revealing the information, but is rather drawn from the enormous input of the collective activity of the human race and the metaphysical energy intelligence input within the cosmos. In 1905, Rabbi Yehudah Ashlag, founder of the Research Centre of Kabbalah in Jerusalem, decoded the mystery of Rabbi Isaac Luria's theories on relativity and parallel universes. Not by coincidence, only then did science in general, and Albert Einstein in particular, begin their revelations of the general relativity theory.

I must not neglect to emphasize that my master never left my side as I wrote this book. I am indebted to him. I would also like to thank my two other teachers, Rabbi Azulai and Shalom Sherabi, whose presence was with me as I wrote the second half of this book. To them, I give my eternal thanks and can only say that being visited by such spiritually evolved beings is a great thrill and honor. My thanks also goes to Rabbi Ashlag, who remained a constant companion to my master during most of these revelations.

I hope that with the information contained in this book, humanity will be empowered to make great strides forward, toward the dream of peace on earth and goodwill toward our fellow men and women. It is a dream that our raised consciousness can bring about.

Let those of us who have kept an open mind throughout this book, now join and rejoice in the revealed secrets on aging and immortality.

God bless us all

ABOUT THE AUTHOR

Rav Berg has been Director of the Kabbalah Centre since 1969, when he assumed leadership from Rabbi Yehuda Tzvi Brandwein. Along with his wife, Karen, Rav Berg opened the doors of the Kabbalah Centre in 1971 to all persons interested in achieving fulfillment, truth and self-improvement through spiritual realization. Under his leadership, the Kabbalah Centre has become an international forum, bringing the wisdom of Kabbalah to the world.

Rav Berg was born in the Williamsburg section of New York City, into a family with a long rabbinical tradition. He studied at Beit Midrash Gavoha in Lakewood, New Jersey, and was ordained at Torah VaDaat, the renowned rabbinical seminary, in Williamsburg. In order to bring the Kabbalah Centre teachings to the English-speaking world, Rav Berg pursued dedicated study of the doctrines of Rav Yehuda Ashlag, the first contemporary Kabbalist and founder of the Kabbalah Centre.

Rav Berg's contributions to the dissemination of Kabbalah include the authorship, editing, translation, and publication of many of its cardinal works, including *Secret Codes of the Universe*, *Wheels of a Soul*, and *The Power of One*. He lectures around the world on the meaning and universal laws of Kabbalah and has met privately with many world leaders encouraging peace in volatile regions. In addition, Rav Berg, along with his sons, Rabbi Yehuda Berg and Rabbi Michael Berg, is directly involved with the instruction of all of the Kabbalah Centre's teachers.

Through Rav Berg's leadership, the Kabbalah Centre has grown to a membership of over 3.4 million students in 39 centres across the world.